Vocabu Riddles

Book 1

A to Z Catastrophes

Vocabulary Riddles series is available in print or eBook form.

Book 1

Book 2

Written by
Diane Hartsig

Edited by
Patricia Gray

Graphic Design by
Scott Slyter

© 2017

THE CRITICAL THINKING CO.™
www.CriticalThinking.com
Phone: 800-458-4849 • Fax: 541-756-1758
1991 Sherman Ave., Suite 200 • North Bend • OR 97459
ISBN 978-1-60144-911-5

MIX
Paper from responsible sources
FSC® C011935

Reproduction of This Copyrighted Material
The intellectual material in this product is the copyrighted property of The Critical Thinking Co.™ The individual or entity who initially purchased this product from The Critical Thinking Co.™ or one of its authorized resellers is licensed to reproduce (print or duplicate on paper) each page of this product for use within one home or one classroom. Our copyright and this limited reproduction permission (user) agreement strictly prohibit the sale of any of the copyrighted material in this product. Any reproduction beyond these expressed limits is strictly prohibited without the written permission of The Critical Thinking Co.™ Please visit http://www.criticalthinking.com/copyright for more information. The Critical Thinking Co.™ retains full intellectual property rights on all its products (eBooks, books, and software).

Printed in the United States of America by McNaughton & Gunn, Inc., Saline, MI (July 2020)

Table of Contents

About This Book

This book offers a collection of fun, alliterative riddles for students in Grades 4 – 8. Ideas for words have come from many sources including the *New York Times* and *The New Yorker*. Decoding the riddles can be an impetus for incorporating dynamic words into students' lexicons and their writing. As a bonus, many of the words appear on ACT and SAT vocabulary lists.

Unlocking each letter's misfortune exposes the reader to four vocabulary words. Some of the words may sound familiar, but to understand the gist of the riddle, all four words are needed. A series of questions after each riddle prompts analysis of the vocabulary. Words are sorted by definition, synonym, antonym, and part of speech.

The last activity asks students to synthesize the meaning of all four vocabulary words. From four sentences, they choose the most fitting representation of the riddle's main idea. To accomplish this, each of the sentence's four synonyms must be evaluated for its compatibility with the riddle's word.

Decoding the Riddles

Here are some helpful hints:

- The best approach is to read through all of the questions before trying to answer any of them. Some of the words are similar in meaning with only nuances between them.
- Pay attention to the part of speech for the synonyms and antonyms as it is another clue.
- To decipher parts of speech, remember verbs ending in the suffix –ing can be gerunds which act as nouns. Verbs ending in the suffixes –ing and –ed can be participles which act as adjectives. Look closely at how the word is used.
- For pronunciation of words and definitions, consult a dictionary.
- Remember, many words have multiple meanings. To select the sentence with the appropriate synonyms, consider the context of the original word.

About The Author

Diane Hartsig earned a journalism degree from Michigan State University and an elementary education degree from Western Michigan University. She is in her eighth year of teaching and is currently a fifth grade teacher in Dowagiac, Michigan. Diane was inspired to write *Vocabulary Riddles A to Z Catastrophes* because she spends so much of her school day interpreting unknown words for students. She lives in Dowagiac with her husband and three children.

© 2017 The Critical Thinking Co.™ • www.CriticalThinking.com • 800-458-4849

A's arrant asperity made him alienated and abhorred.

1. Which word means "to feel hatred or loathing for?" ____________
2. "Unmitigated" is a synonym for which word? ____________
3. "Amiability" is an antonym for which word? ____________
4. Which word means "to make isolated?" ____________
5. "Abhorred" is used as what part of speech? noun verb adjective adverb
6. Choose the sentence that best decodes the riddle.
   a. A's undue loudness made him unpopular and deplored.
   b. A's extreme harshness made him estranged and resented.
   c. A's absolute bitterness made him miserable and detested.
   d. A's profound ignorance made him disillusioned and despised.

Despite the admonishments, an audacious A ambled into the abyss.

1. Which word means "a scolding or rebuke?" ____________
2. "Chasm" is a synonym for which word? ____________
3. "Yielding" is an antonym for which word? ____________
4. Which word means "to walk or move at a slow pace?" ____________
5. "Audacious" is used as what part of speech? noun verb adjective adverb
6. Choose the sentence that best decodes the riddle.
   a. In spite of the warning, anxious A wandered into the hole.
   b. With no regard to the directions, senseless A bounded into the emptiness.
   c. Disregarding the lecture, shameless A romped into the confusion.
   d. In defiance of the advice, brash A strolled into the crevasse.

© 2017 The Critical Thinking Co.™ • www.CriticalThinking.com • 800-458-4849

Boisterous bunkum and ballyhoo befuddled B.

1. Which word means “foolish talk or nonsense?” ____________________
2. “Rollicking” is a synonym for which word? ____________________
3. “Enlightened” is an antonym for which word? ____________________
4. Which word means “extravagant fuss?” ____________________
5. “Befuddled” is used as what part of speech? noun verb adjective adverb
6. Choose the sentence that best decodes the riddle.

    a. Annoying drivel and outbursts ruffled B.

    b. Rowdy foolishness and hoopla bamboozled B.

    c. Ceaseless blather and racket discomfited B.

    d. Mindless blather and commotion enthralled B.

Because B was a member of the beau monde and not a bourgeois, barbarous acts bewildered her.

1. Which word means “the world of high society?” ____________________
2. “Mystified” is a synonym for which word? ____________________
3. “Civilized” is an antonym for which word? ____________________
4. Which word means “a member of the middle class?” ____________________
5. “Bewildered” is used as what part of speech? noun verb adjective adverb
6. Choose the sentence that best decodes the riddle.

    a. Because B was a member of the jet set and not a commoner, oafish deeds grated her.

    b. Because B was sophisticated and not one of the masses, rude behavior disenchanted her.

    c. Because B was part of the elite class and not one of the multitudes, crude actions flummoxed her.

    d. Because B was wealthy and not ordinary, coarse things distressed her.

© 2017 The Critical Thinking Co.™ • www.CriticalThinking.com • 800-458-4849

To his chagrin, C capitulated when his contrivance couldn't crack the conundrum.

1. Which word means "a scheme or plan?" ________________
2. "Enigma" is a synonym for which word? ________________
3. "Exultation" is an antonym for which word? ________________
4. Which word means "to give up or surrender?" ________________
5. "Chagrin" is used as what part of speech? noun verb adjective adverb
6. Choose the sentence that best decodes the riddle.

    a. To his displeasure, C conceded when his tactics couldn't unravel the mystery.

    b. To his vexation, C floundered when his maneuvers couldn't resolve the problem.

    c. To his disgrace, C relented when his exploits couldn't rectify the situation.

    d. To his distress, C sputtered when his pursuits couldn't make progress on the challenge.

Contumacious C was castigated because his calumny caused consternation.

1. Which word means "utter confusion and dismay?" ________________
2. "Chastised" is a synonym for which word? ________________
3. "Subordinate" is an antonym for which word? ________________
4. Which word means "false statements damaging another's reputation?" ________________
5. "Contumacious" is used as what part of speech? noun verb adjective adverb
6. Choose the sentence that best decodes the riddle.

    a. Willful C was removed because his character assassination caused chaos.

    b. Disobedient C was demoted because his gossiping caused a disruption.

    c. Wicked C was punished because his behavior caused violence.

    d. Defiant C was scolded because his slander caused an uproar.

© 2017 The Critical Thinking Co.™ • www.CriticalThinking.com • 800-458-4849

A deluge of disparaging discourse disconcerted D.

1. Which word means "an overwhelming amount?" ____________________
2. "Rhetoric" is a synonym for which word? ____________________
3. "Commendatory" is an antonym for which word? ____________________
4. Which word means "to perturb or ruffle?" ____________________
5. "Disconcerted" is used as what part of speech? noun verb adjective adverb
6. Choose the sentence that best decodes the riddle.
   a. A flood of belittling dialogue rattled D.
   b. A torrent of stinging insults ridiculed D.
   c. A sequence of hostile comments harried D.
   d. A series of awkward discussions discomposed D.

D was the denizen of a deplorably dilapidated domicile.

1. Which word means "inhabitant or occupant?" ____________________
2. "Abode" is a synonym for which word? ____________________
3. "Maintained" is an antonym for which word? ____________________
4. Which word means "shockingly bad?" ____________________
5. "Deplorably" is used as what part of speech? noun verb adjective adverb
6. Choose the sentence that best decodes the riddle.
   a. D was the tenant of an appallingly bad residence.
   b. D was the dweller of shamelessly inadequate quarters.
   c. D was the resident of woefully neglected lodging.
   d. D was the owner of an insufficiently constructed home.

© 2017 The Critical Thinking Co.™ • www.CriticalThinking.com • 800-458-4849

E's explication of the egregious embezzlement was not efficacious.

1. Which word means "the misuse of money entrusted to one's care?" ____________
2. "Potent" is a synonym for which word? ____________
3. "Marvelous" is an antonym for which word? ____________
4. Which word means "a detailed explanation?" ____________
5. "Embezzlement" is used as what part of speech? noun verb adjective adverb
6. Choose the sentence that best decodes the riddle.
   a. E's report of the outrageous theft was not lengthy.
   b. E's version of the shocking crime was not detailed.
   c. E's account of the blatant fraud was not clear.
   d. E's testimony of the glaring theft was not persuasive.

E evacuated after her enterprising endeavors ended erratically.

1. Which word means "moving unpredictably?" ____________
2. "Abandoned" is a synonym for which word? ____________
3. "Lethargic" is an antonym for which word? ____________
4. Which word means "an effort with a purpose?" ____________
5. "Erratically" is used as what part of speech? noun verb adjective adverb
6. Choose the sentence that best decodes the riddle.
   a. E departed when her ambitious attempts ended haphazardly.
   b. E withdrew when her creative proposal ended abitrarily.
   c. E vacated when her resourceful scheme ended abruptly.
   d. E retreated when her inventive undertakings ended recklessly.

© 2017 The Critical Thinking Co.™ • www.CriticalThinking.com • 800-458-4849

Flagitious F was fulminated for causing fervor and fracases.

1. Which word means "intense feelings?" ____________________
2. "Denounced" is a synonym for which word? ____________________
3. "Virtuous" is an antonym for which word? ____________________
4. Which word means "a quarrel or brawl?" ____________________
5. "Fervor" is used as what part of speech? noun verb adjective adverb
6. Choose the sentence that best decodes the riddle.

   a. Wicked F was condemned for causing vehemence and altercations.

   b. Scandalous F was penalized for causing an uproar and conflicts.

   c. Mischievous F was criticized for causing a ruckus and disputes.

   d. Immature F was removed for causing a commotion and skirmishes.

Fretful F was fraught with fatuity and foibles.

1. Which word means "stupidity or foolishness?" ____________________
2. "Apprehensive" is a synonym for which word? ____________________
3. "Virtue" is an antonym for which word? ____________________
4. Which word means "filled with difficulties?" ____________________
5. "Fraught" is used as what part of speech? noun verb adjective adverb
6. Choose the sentence that best decodes the riddle.

   a. Rascally F was preoccupied with foolery and capers.

   b. Agitated F was rife with idiocy and weakness.

   c. Weak F was distracted by lunacy and missteps.

   d. Muddled F was concerned with insanity and vices.

© 2017 The Critical Thinking Co.™ • www.CriticalThinking.com • 800-458-4849

G's gallivanting in garish garb was a gaffe.

1. Which word means "to move about for pleasure?" ____________
2. "Faux pas" is a synonym for which word? ____________
3. "Conservative" is an antonym for which word? ____________
4. Which word means "distinct clothing?" ____________
5. "Gallivanting" is used as what part of speech? noun verb adjective adverb
6. Choose the sentence that best decodes the riddle.

   a. G's dancing in flashy attire was a spectacle.

   b. G's flitting in hideous costume was a mistake.

   c. G's jaunting in dreadful apparel was a mortification.

   d. G's traipsing in a loud outfit was a blunder.

G glowered after he was gibed for being a gauche gormandizer.

1. Which word means "to tease or taunt?" ____________
2. "Scowled" is a synonym for which word? ____________
3. "Sophisticated" is an antonym for which word? ____________
4. What word means "one who eats greedily?" ____________
5. "Gauche" is used as what part of speech? noun verb adjective adverb
6. Choose the sentence that best decodes the riddle.

   a. G bristled after he was reprimanded for being a crude overeater.

   b. G glared after he was ridiculed for being a graceless glutton.

   c. G gaped after he was mocked for being a clumsy gorger.

   d. G frowned after he was lectured for being an inconsiderate pig.

© 2017 The Critical Thinking Co.™ • www.CriticalThinking.com • 800-458-4849

Full of hubris, haughty H couldn't hew to the hoi polloi.

1. Which word means "to conform?" ____________________
2. "Pompous" is a synonym for which word? ____________________
3. "Modesty" is an antonym for which word? ____________________
4. Which word means "the general population?" ____________________
5. "Hubris" is used as what part of speech? noun verb adjective adverb
6. Choose the sentence that best decodes the riddle.
    a. Full of vanity, sophisticated H couldn't associate with the commoners.
    b. Full of arrogance, highfalutin H couldn't adapt to the populace.
    c. Full of superiority, uppity H couldn't mingle with the masses.
    d. Full of conceit, pretentious H couldn't identify with the multitude.

H caused hugger-mugger with a harangue full of harum-scarum hokum.

1. Which word means "a long aggressive speech?" ____________________
2. "Blather" is a synonym for which word? ____________________
3. "Responsible" is an antonym for which word? ____________________
4. Which word means "a confusion?" ____________________
5. "Hugger-mugger" is used as what part of speech? noun verb adjective adverb
6. Choose the sentence that best decodes the riddle.
    a. H caused disorder with a rant full of reckless rubbish.
    b. H caused a brawl with a tirade full of aggressive tommyrot.
    c. H caused havoc with a lecture full of contentious sentiment.
    d. H caused a muddle with a sermon full of irresponsible barbs.

© 2017 The Critical Thinking Co.™ • www.CriticalThinking.com • 800-458-4849

Imperiled by an imbroglio, impuissant I reached an impasse.

1. Which word means “a difficult situation?” ____________________
2. “Jeopardized” is a synonym for which word? ____________________
3. “Potent” is an antonym for which word? ____________________
4. Which word means “a situation in which no progress can be made?” ____________________
5. “Imperiled” is used as what part of speech? noun verb adjective adverb
6. Choose the sentence that best decodes the riddle.

    a. Endangered by a predicament, weak I reached a conclusion.

    b. Deterred by a setback, demoralized I reached a deadlock.

    c. Compromised by a complication, powerless I reached a stalemate.

    d. Negated by a quandary, inept I reached a standstill.

Incorrigible I tried to impede the inquisition into his incivility.

1. Which word means “intensive questioning?” ____________________
2. “Obstruct” is a synonym for which word? ____________________
3. “Remediable” is an antonym for which word? ____________________
4. Which word means “rude behavior?” ____________________
5. “Incorrigible” is used as what part of speech? noun verb adjective adverb
6. Choose the sentence that best decodes the riddle.

    a. Habitual I tried to hinder the probe into his high jinks.

    b. Unreformed I tried to halt the hearing into his depravity.

    c. Chronic I tried to hobble the inquiry into his curtness.

    d. Incurable I tried to inhibit the interrogation into his insolence.

© 2017 The Critical Thinking Co.™ • www.CriticalThinking.com • 800-458-4849

J's juvenile jeering jarred the jocund crowd's jollity.

1. Which word means "insulting remarks?" ______________
2. "Puerile" is a synonym for which word? ______________
3. "Crestfallen" is an antonym for which word? ______________
4. Which word means "cheerful activity?" ______________
5. "Jeering" is used as what part of speech? noun verb adjective adverb
6. Choose the sentence that best decodes the riddle.

   a. J's immature mocking suspended the exuberant crowd's shindig.

   b. J's childish jesting interrupted the festive crowd's celebration.

   c. J's adolescent taunting disturbed the merry crowd's revelry.

   d. J's crude heckling derailed the vivacious crowd's frolicking.

J's jejune jabberwocky was juxtaposed with his jargon.

1. Which word means "technical terminology?" ______________
2. "Drivel" is a synonym for which word? ______________
3. "Intriguing" is an antonym for which word? ______________
4. Which word means "to place side by side?" ______________
5. "Juxtaposed" is used as what part of speech? noun verb adjective adverb
6. Choose the sentence that best decodes the riddle.

   a. J's stodgy gibberish contrasted with his shoptalk.

   b. J's humdrum babble was coupled with his lingo.

   c. J's doltish prattle differed from his vocabulary.

   d. J's cockeyed mumbo jumbo was contrary to his dialect.

© 2017 The Critical Thinking Co.™ • www.CriticalThinking.com • 800-458-4849

Knackered K couldn't kibitz with kindred spirits at the klatch.

1. Which word means "a social, casual gathering?" ____________
2. "Conversate" is a synonym for which word? ____________
3. "Invigorated" is an antonym for which word? ____________
4. Which word means "similar in kind?" ____________
5. "Kibitz" is used as what part of speech? noun verb adjective adverb
6. Choose the sentence that best decodes the riddle.
   a. Slumberous K couldn't schmooze with matching spirits at the party.
   b. Fatigued K couldn't chat with affiliated spirits at the get-together.
   c. Dispassionate K couldn't jabber with familiar spirits at the function.
   d. Indisposed K couldn't blab with related spirits at the event.

Kittle K's kvetching about the koan created a kerfuffle.

1. Which word means "a paradoxical riddle?" ____________
2. "Erratic" is a synonym for which word? ____________
3. "Tranquility" is an antonym for which word? ____________
4. Which word means "to complain?" ____________
5. "Kittle" is used as what part of speech? noun verb adjective adverb
6. Choose the sentence that best decodes the riddle.
   a. Irksome K's whining about the problem created a fray.
   b. Touchy K's griping about the puzzle created a commotion.
   c. Nettling K's bemoaning of the mystery created a furor.
   d. Dithery K's bellyaching about the challenge created a ruckus.

© 2017 The Critical Thinking Co.™ • www.CriticalThinking.com • 800-458-4849

Logy L lolled with languor during the longueur.

1. Which word means “a dull and tedious piece of writing?” ____________
2. “Weary” is a synonym for which word? ____________
3. “Vigor” is an antonym for which word? ____________
4. Which word means “to act in a lazy manner?” ____________
5. “Logy” is used as what part of speech? noun verb adjective adverb
6. Choose the sentence that best decodes the riddle.

   a. Groggy L slouched with listlessness during the book’s longsome parts.

   b. Sluggish L drooped with lethargy during the book’s inert parts.

   c. Apathetic L slumped with fatigue during the book’s leaden parts.

   d. Limp L crumpled with idleness during the book’s prolonged parts.

A lachrymose L lamented over the litany of losses from the larceny.

1. Which word means “a lengthy recitation?” ____________
2. “Weepy” is a synonym for which word? ____________
3. “Rejoiced” is an antonym for which word? ____________
4. Which word means “the wrongful taking of personal property?” ____________
5. “Litany” is used as what part of speech? noun verb adjective adverb
6. Choose the sentence that best decodes the riddle.

   a. A woeful L whined about the substantial losses from the theft.

   b. A forlorn L rued the accumulated losses from the banditry.

   c. A melancholy L fretted over the considerable losses from the thievery.

   d. A tearful L bewailed the elongated list of losses from the robbery.

© 2017 The Critical Thinking Co.™ • www.CriticalThinking.com • 800-458-4849

Mendacious M's malady manifested after his malingering.

1. Which word means "to pretend illness to avoid duty?" ____________________
2. "Ailment" is a synonym for which word? ____________________
3. "Veracious" is an antonym for which word? ____________________
4. Which word means "to display or become obvious?" ____________________
5. "Manifested" is used as what part of speech? noun verb adjective adverb
6. Choose the sentence that best decodes the riddle.
   a. Duplicitous M's disease materialized after he fabricated a disorder to dodge his tasks.
   b. Deceitful M's health degenerated after a sham sickness to circumvent his chores.
   c. Compunctious M became ill after he feigned a disorder to shirk his responsibilities.
   d. Cagey M's affliction worsened after a bogus illness to evade obligations.

The magistrate placed Machiavellian M in manacles for his mulcting.

1. Which word means "one who administers laws?" ____________________
2. "Shackles" is a synonym for which word? ____________________
3. "Scrupulous" is an antonym for which word? ____________________
4. Which word means "to obtain by fraudulent means?" ____________________
5. "Manacles" is used as what part of speech? noun verb adjective adverb
6. Choose the sentence that best decodes the riddle.
   a. The judge placed truculent M in chains for his hustling.
   b. The arbiter placed deleterious M in irons for his swindling.
   c. The bailiff placed devious M in fetters for his defrauding.
   d. The court placed debased M in restraints for his conning.

© 2017 The Critical Thinking Co.™ • www.CriticalThinking.com • 800-458-4849

N's narcissism necessitated her to have a nimiety of nugatory things.

1. Which word means "to compel?" ____________________
2. "Frivolous" is a synonym for which word? ____________________
3. "Moderation" is an antonym for which word? ____________________
4. Which word means "excessive interest in oneself?" ____________________
5. "Necessitated" is used as what part of speech? noun verb adjective adverb
6. Choose the sentence that best decodes the riddle.
    a. N's vanity entailed a preposterous amount of obtuse things.
    b. N's pomposity pressed her to have an exorbitance of inferior things.
    c. N's egotism warranted a superfluous amount of trivial things.
    d. N's self-regard emboldened her to have a plethora of futile things.

N was nescient of her nimble nemesis's noxious ways.

1. Which word means "quick to understand?" ____________________
2. "Adversary" is a synonym for which word? ____________________
3. "Benign" is an antonym for which word? ____________________
4. Which word means "lacking awareness?" ____________________
5. "Noxious" is used as what part of speech? noun verb adjective adverb
6. Choose the sentence that best decodes the riddle.
    a. N was incognizant of her resourceful rival's baneful ways.
    b. N was heedless of her meticulous enemy's cunning ways.
    c. N was oblivious of her apt opponent's pernicious ways.
    d. N was ignorant of her nefarious foe's insidious ways.

© 2017 The Critical Thinking Co.™ • www.CriticalThinking.com • 800-458-4849

No one oppugned when opprobrious O was placed in an oubliette for his odious behavior.

1. Which word means "to question or fight against?" ____________
2. "Infamous" is a synonym for which word? ____________
3. "Innocuous" is an antonym for which word? ____________
4. Which word means "a dungeon with only an opening at the top?" ____________
5. "Opprobrious" is used as what part of speech? noun verb adjective adverb
6. Choose the sentence that best decodes the riddle.

   a. No one dissented when felonious O was imprisoned for his rancid behavior.

   b. No one protested when disreputable O was imprisoned for his repugnant behavior.

   c. No one demurred when indicted O was imprisoned for his insufferable behavior.

   d. No one remonstrated when notorious O was imprisoned for his illicit behavior.

Otiose O obstinately obviated every onerous task.

1. Which word means "to reduce or prevent?" ____________
2. "Burdensome" is a synonym for which word? ____________
3. "Productive" is an antonym for which word? ____________
4. Which word means "stubborn or difficult to manage? ____________
5. "Obstinately" is used as what part of speech? noun verb adjective adverb
6. Choose the sentence that best decodes the riddle.

   a. Mulish O willfully thwarted every weighty task.

   b. Slothful O steadily stymied every strenuous task.

   c. Idle O doggedly deflected every demoralizing task.

   d. Indolent O tenaciously averted every oppressive task.

© 2017 The Critical Thinking Co.™ • www.CriticalThinking.com • 800-458-4849

The palisade was a palatable solution for palliating threats and pacifying P.

1. Which word means "to make less severe?" ________________
2. "Adequate" is a synonym for which word? ________________
3. "Infuriating" is an antonym for which word? ________________
4. Which word means "a defensive fence of wooden stakes?" ________________
5. "Palliating" is used as what part of speech? noun verb adjective adverb
6. Choose the sentence that best decodes the riddle.
   a. The fort was a salient solution for dismissing threats and disarming P.
   b. The enclosure was a compulsory solution for curtailing threats and placating P.
   c. The stockade was a copacetic solution for abating threats and allaying P.
   d. The barrier was a requisite solution for diluting threats and appeasing P.

Peccant P's penchant for pilfering was a perfidy.

1. Which word means "guilty of sinning?" ________________
2. "Affinity" is a synonym for which word? ________________
3. "Fidelity" is an antonym for which word? ________________
4. Which word means "to repeatedly steal small amounts?" ________________
5. "Pilfering" is used as what part of speech? noun verb adjective adverb
6. Choose the sentence that best decodes the riddle.
   a. Corrupt P's leanings toward looting were a laxity.
   b. Erring P's inclinations for lifting were an infidelity.
   c. Impetuous P's flair for filching was a falseness.
   d. Deceitful P's pattern of pinching was a disloyalty.

© 2017 The Critical Thinking Co.™ • www.CriticalThinking.com • 800-458-4849

Q's query about the quagmire did little to quell her qualms.

1. Which word means "a question?" ____________
2. "Predicament" is a synonym for which word? ____________
3. "Agitate" is an antonym for which word? ____________
4. Which word means "a feeling of uneasiness?" ____________
5. "Quell" is used as what part of speech? noun verb adjective adverb
6. Choose the sentence that best decodes the riddle.

   a. Q's inquiry into the impasse did little to repress her reluctance.

   b. Q's probe into the perplexity did little to calm her compunction.

   c. Q's research into the bemusement did little to rectify her reservations.

   d. Q's study of the stalemate didn't dampen her distrust.

Querulous Q needed a quietus to stop quibbling after the quarrel.

1. Which word means "to make objections about minor matters?" ____________
2. "Altercation" is a synonym for which word? ____________
3. "Affable" is an antonym for which word? ____________
4. Which word means "something that suppresses?" ____________
5. "Querulous" is used as what part of speech? noun verb adjective adverb
6. Choose the sentence that best decodes the riddle.

   a. Snappish Q needed a repose to stop spouting after the spat.

   b. Crabby Q needed a release to stop carping after the clash.

   c. Cranky Q needed an exemption to stop clamoring after the controversy.

   d. Raspy Q needed a respite to stop fuming after the feud.

© 2017 The Critical Thinking Co.™ • www.CriticalThinking.com • 800-458-4849

Rife with rancor, R's reprehensible behavior rankled the town.

1. Which word means "deserving condemnation?" ____________________
2. "Enraged" is a synonym for which word? ____________________
3. "Amity" is an antonym for which word? ____________________
4. Which word means "full of or abounding with?" ____________________
5. "Rife" is used as what part of speech? noun verb adjective adverb
6. Choose the sentence that best decodes the riddle.

   a. Replete with bitterness, R's atrocious behavior appalled the town.

   b. Teeming with hostility, R's culpable behavior incensed the town.

   c. Awash with detriment, R's menacing behavior vexed the town.

   d. Abounding with disdain, R's horrendous behavior infuriated the town.

R renounced his recalcitrance but soon recidivated back to his repugnant ways.

1. Which word means "stubborn defiance of authority?" ____________________
2. "Abdicated" is a synonym for which word? ____________________
3. "Inoffensive" is an antonym for which word? ____________________
4. Which word means "to regress back to bad behavior?" ____________________
5. "Recidivated" is used as what part of speech? noun verb adjective adverb
6. Choose the sentence that best decodes the riddle.

   a. R ceded his balkiness but soon relapsed back to his baneful ways.

   b. R rescinded his knavery but soon ebbed back to his roguish ways.

   c. R concluded his contrariness but soon lapsed back to his contemptible ways.

   d. R relinquished his contumacy but soon reverted back to his repulsive ways.

© 2017 The Critical Thinking Co.™ • www.CriticalThinking.com • 800-458-4849

Senescent S had a salient sallowness and a lack of salubriousness.

1. Which word means "promoting health?" ____________
2. "Conspicuous" is a synonym for which word? ____________
3. "Youthful" is an antonym for which word? ____________
4. Which word means "a yellowish color of the skin?" ____________
5. "Salubriousness" is used as what part of speech? noun verb adjective adverb
6. Choose the sentence that best decodes the riddle.

    a. Geriatric S had a striking pastiness and a lack of stamina.

    b. Ancient S had a prominent wanness and a lack of vibrancy.

    c. Aging S had a conspicuous pallidity and a lack of vigor.

    d. Elderly S had a notable jaundice and a lack of hardiness.

S solicitously scoffed at the spurious charges of sortilege.

1. Which word means "in an anxious or worried manner?" ____________
2. "Dismissed" is a synonym for which word? ____________
3. "Authentic" is an antonym for which word? ____________
4. Which word means "sorcery or witchcraft?" ____________
5. "Solicitously" is used as what part of speech? noun verb adjective adverb
6. Choose the sentence that best decodes the riddle.

    a. S categorically scorned the flawed charge of bewitchment.

    b. S emphatically contemned the bogus charge of enchantment.

    c. S apprehensively derided the false charge of wizardry.

    d. S soundly spurned the erroneous charge of devilry.

© 2017 The Critical Thinking Co.™ • www.CriticalThinking.com • 800-458-4849

T's temerity led him to traduce others in tumultuous tirades.

1. Which word means "a long, angry and accusatory speech?" ____________
2. "Malign" is a synonym for which word? ____________
3. "Wariness" is an antonym for which word? ____________
4. Which word means "loud, excited and emotional?" ____________
5. "Tumultuous" is used as what part of speech? noun verb adjective adverb
6. Choose the sentence that best decodes the riddle.
   a. T's pomposity led him to slander others in rowdy rants.
   b. T's gall led him to defame others in frenzied diatribes.
   c. T's pertness led him to chastise others in thunderous criticisms.
   d. T's impudence led him to lambaste others in obscene onslaughts.

After the trouncing, a tumid and timorous T was feeling torpid.

1. Which word means "a severe thrashing?" ____________
2. "Lethargic" is a synonym for which word? ____________
3. "Audacious" is an antonym for which word? ____________
4. Which word means "swollen?" ____________
5. "Trouncing" is used as what part of speech? noun verb adjective adverb
6. Choose the sentence that best decodes the riddle.
   a. After the drubbing, a puffed and skittish T was feeling sluggish.
   b. After the licking, a bloated and vanquished T was feeling inert.
   c. After the whipping, a distended and tremulous T was feeling subdued.
   d. After the shellacking, a contused and crushed T was feeling feeble.

© 2017 The Critical Thinking Co.™ • www.CriticalThinking.com • 800-458-4849

Unfettered by urbane behavior, unregenerate U continued her uncouthness.

1. Which word means "crudeness or awkwardness?" ________________
2. "Uninhibited" is a synonym for which word? ________________
3. "Boorish" is an antonym for which word? ________________
4. Which word means "sinful or not reformed?" ________________
5. "Unfettered" is used as what part of speech? noun verb adjective adverb
6. Choose the sentence that best decodes the riddle.
   a. Unchecked by cultivated behavior, stubborn U continued her crudity.
   b. Unconstrained by refined behavior, unrepentant U continued her coarseness.
   c. Uncontrolled by appropriate behavior, implacable U continued her crudeness.
   d. Unrestricted by customary behavior, unswerving U continued her churlishness.

U remained unflappable and unerring during the unprecedented upheaval.

1. Which word means "not easily upset?" ________________
2. "Tumult" is a synonym for which word? ________________
3. "Fallible" is an antonym for which word? ________________
4. Which word means "not experienced before?" ________________
5. "Unerring" is used as what part of speech? noun verb adjective adverb
6. Choose the sentence that best decodes the riddle.
   a. U remained flawless and coherent during the unusual turbulence.
   b. U remained levelheaded and impeccable during the unmatched pandemonium.
   c. U remained absolute and credible during the exceptional cataclysm.
   d. U remained rational and poised during the unrivaled chaos.

© 2017 The Critical Thinking Co.™ • www.CriticalThinking.com • 800-458-4849

V was vitiated by voluptuary pursuits and every vestige of his villatic upbringing was gone.

1. Which word means "concerned with luxury and pleasure?" ________________
2. "Tarnished" is a synonym for which word? ________________
3. "Urban" is an antonym for which word? ________________
4. Which word means "the smallest trace?" ________________
5. "Villatic" is used as what part of speech? noun verb adjective adverb
6. Choose the sentence that best decodes the riddle.
   a. V was transformed by illustrious pursuits and every bit of his bucolic upbringing was gone.
   b. V was engrossed with wanton pursuits and every wisp of his rural upbringing was gone.
   c. V was perverted by unseemly pursuits and every sliver of his rustic upbringing was gone.
   d. V was debased by indulgent pursuits and every remnant of his pastoral upbringing was gone.

V was vociferously vituperated for her velleity for veracity.

1. Which word means "a weak desire?" ________________
2. "Castigated" is a synonym for which word? ________________
3. "Deceitfulness" is an antonym for which word? ________________
4. Which word means "in a clamorous manner?" ________________
5. "Vociferously" is used as what part of speech? noun verb adjective adverb
6. Choose the sentence that best decodes the riddle.
   a. V was shrilly assailed for her weak impulse for sincerity.
   b. V was searingly scathed for her weak urge for probity.
   c. V was savagely slammed for her weak commitment for verity.
   d. V was raucously disparaged for her weak devotion to integrity.

© 2017 The Critical Thinking Co.™ • www.CriticalThinking.com • 800-458-4849

The weary wayfarer, W, didn't care one whit about being waylaid.

1. Which word means "one who travels, especially on foot?" __________
2. "Iota" is a synonym for which word? __________
3. "Invigorated" is an antonym for which word? __________
4. Which word means "to stop or interrupt?" __________
5. "Whit" is used as what part of speech? noun verb adjective adverb
6. Choose the sentence that best decodes the riddle.

    a. The ragged roamer didn't care one atom about being accosted.

    b. The prostrate drifter didn't care one speck about being detained.

    c. The languid vagabond didn't care one lick about being intercepted.

    d. The groggy nomad didn't care one hoot about being high-jacked.

The waggery whetted wily W's waywardness.

1. Which word means "to make more keen?" __________
2. "Recalcitrance" is a synonym for which word? __________
3. "Guileless" is an antonym for which word? __________
4. Which word means "playful behavior not intended to do harm?" __________
5. "Whetted" is used as what part of speech? noun verb adjective adverb
6. Choose the sentence that best decodes the riddle.

    a. The impishness aroused artful W's insubordination.

    b. The rascality kindled canny W's impertinence.

    c. The roguery rejuvenated rakish W's peevishness.

    d. The antics animated crafty W's capriciousness.

© 2017 The Critical Thinking Co.™ • www.CriticalThinking.com • 800-458-4849

Because of her xenophobia, the xanthous Xanthippe was not xenial to X.

1. Which word means “a scolding woman?” ________________

2. “Congenial” is a synonym of which word? ________________

3. “Multiculturalism” is an antonym for which word? ________________

4. Which word means “having yellow, red or auburn hair and a light complexion?”

   ____

5. “Xenial” is used as what part of speech? noun verb adjective adverb

6. Choose the sentence that best decodes the riddle.

   a. Because of her prejudice, the amber-haired ogress was not genteel to X.

   b. Because of her isolationism, the auburn-haired hag was not decorous to X.

   c. Because of her ethnocentrism, the pale harridan was not extroverted with X.

   d. Because of her nationalism, the blond shrew was not hospitable to X.

X’s xenomania led him to a xenodochium with a xystus in a xeric area.

1. Which word means “an intense fondness for anything foreign?” ________________

2. “Hotel” is a synonym for which word? ________________

3. “Hydric” is an antonym for which word? ________________

4. Which word means “a covered porch for exercising?” ________________

5. “Xeric” is used as what part of speech? noun verb adjective adverb

6. Choose the sentence that best decodes the riddle.

   a. X’s forage for foreign things led him to lodging with a vestibule in a parched area.

   b. X’s fidelity to foreign things led him to an inn with a terrace in a barren area.

   c. X’s focus on foreign things led him to a resort with a veranda in a torrid area.

   d. X’s fetish for foreign things led him to a hostel with a portico in an arid area.

© 2017 The Critical Thinking Co.™ • www.CriticalThinking.com • 800-458-4849

Y, a yokel, yammered on about yeasty yearnings.

1. Which word means "a naïve person living in a nonurban area?" ______________
2. "Pinings" is a synonym for which word? ______________
3. "Sober" is an antonym for which word? ______________
4. Which word means "to persistently talk?" ______________
5. "Yammered" is used as what part of speech? noun verb adjective adverb
6. Choose the sentence that best decodes the riddle.

   a. Y, a bumpkin, blabbed about harebrained hankerings.

   b. Y, a hillbilly, gabbed about elaborate longings.

   c. Y, a peasant, prated about petty cravings.

   d. Y, a provincial, chatted about giddy gambits.

As the yeti appeared yonder on the hill, a yielding Y yawped.

1. Which word means "abominable snowman?" ______________
2. "Bawled" is a synonym for which word? ______________
3. "Resistant" is an antonym for which word? ______________
4. Which word means "in a distant place but usually within sight?" ______________
5. "Yonder" is used as what part of speech? noun verb adjective adverb
6. Choose the sentence that best decodes the riddle.

   a. As the mythical creature appeared past the hill, a craven Y screeched.

   b. As the legendary creature appeared on the hill, a docile Y bayed.

   c. As the folklore creature appeared beyond the hill, a passive Y squawked.

   d. As the fabled creature appeared over the hill, an overwrought Y squealed.

© 2017 The Critical Thinking Co.™ • www.CriticalThinking.com • 800-458-4849

Z became zappy when the zealot's zest hit a zenith.

1. Which word means "lively or energetic?" ____________
2. "Pinnacle" is a synonym for which word? ____________
3. "Apathy" is an antonym for which word? ____________
4. Which word means "a person with a fanatical devotion to a cause?" ____________
5. "Zenith" is used as what part of speech? noun verb adjective adverb
6. Choose the sentence that best decodes the riddle.
   a. Z became euphoric when the crusader's keenness hit a crest.
   b. Z became buoyant when the ideologue's exuberance hit a climax.
   c. Z became animated when the extremist's aspiration hit a crescendo.
   d. Z became blissful when the radical's ardor hit an apex.

During the zephyr, Z zanily zipped onto the zeppelin.

1. Which word means "a gentle breeze?" ____________
2. "Careened" is a synonym for which word? ____________
3. "Prudently" is an antonym for which word? ____________
4. Which word means "an early airship?" ____________
5. "Zanily" is used as what part of speech? noun verb adjective adverb
6. Choose the sentence that best decodes the riddle.
   a. During the draft, Z awkwardly dashed onto the dirigible.
   b. During the breath, Z daftly barreled onto the blimp.
   c. During the gust, Z clumsily scuttled onto the vessel.
   d. During the gale, Z wackily whizzed onto the balloon.

© 2017 The Critical Thinking Co.™ • www.CriticalThinking.com • 800-458-4849

Answers

Page 1

1. abhorred
2. arrant
3. asperity
4. alienated
5. adjective
6. b. A's extreme harshness made him estranged and resented.

1. admonishments
2. abyss
3. audacious
4. ambled
5. adjective
6. d. In defiance of the advice, brash A strolled into the crevasse.

Page 2

1. bunkum
2. boisterous
3. befuddled
4. ballyhoo
5. verb
6. b. Rowdy foolishness and hoopla bamboozled B.

1. beau monde
2. bewildered
3. barbarous
4. bourgeois
5. verb
6. c. Because B was part of the elite class and not one of the multitudes, crude actions flummoxed her.

Page 3

1. contrivance
2. conundrum
3. chagrin
4. capitulated
5. noun
6. a. To his displeasure, C conceded when his tactics couldn't unravel the mystery.

1. consternation
2. castigated
3. contumacious
4. calumny
5. adjective
6. d. Defiant C was scolded because his slander caused an uproar.

Page 4

1. deluge
2. discourse
3. disparaging
4. disconcerted
5. verb
6. a. A flood of belittling dialogue rattled D.

1. denizen
2. domicile
3. dilapidated
4. deplorably
5. adverb
6. c. D was the resident of woefully neglected lodging.

Page 5

1. embezzlement
2. efficacious
3. egregious
4. explication
5. noun
6. c. E's account of the blatant fraud was not clear.

1. erratically
2. evacuated
3. enterprising
4. endeavors
5. adverb
6. a. E departed when her ambitious attempts ended haphazardly.

Page 6

1. fervor
2. fulminated
3. flagitious
4. fracases
5. noun
6. a. Wicked F was condemned for causing vehemence and altercations.

1. fatuity
2. fretful
3. foibles
4. fraught
5. adjective
6. b. Agitated F was rife with idiocy and weakness.

Page 7

1. gallivanting
2. gaffe
3. garish
4. garb
5. noun
6. d. G's traipsing in a loud outfit was a blunder.

1. gibed
2. glowered
3. gauche
4. gormandizer
5. adjective
6. b. G glared after he was ridiculed for being a graceless glutton.

Page 8

1. hew
2. haughty
3. hubris
4. hoi polloi
5. noun
6. b. Full of arrogance, highfalutin H couldn't adapt to the populace.

1. harangue
2. hokum
3. harum-scarum
4. hugger-mugger
5. noun
6. a. H caused disorder with a rant full of reckless rubbish.

Page 9

1. imbroglio
2. imperiled
3. impuissant
4. impasse
5. adjective
6. c. Compromised by a complication, powerless I reached a stalemate.

1. inquisition
2. impede
3. incorrigible
4. incivility
5. adjective
6. d. Incurable I tried to inhibit the interrogation into his insolence.

Page 10

1. jeering
2. juvenile
3. jocund
4. jollity
5. noun
6. c. J's adolescent taunting disturbed the merry crowd's revelry.

1. jargon
2. jabberwocky
3. jejune
4. juxtaposed
5. verb
6. a. J's stodgy gibberish contrasted with his shoptalk.

Page 11

1. klatch
2. kibitz
3. knackered
4. kindred
5. verb
6. b. Fatigued K couldn't chat with affiliated spirits at the get-together.

1. koan
2. kittle
3. kerfuffle
4. kvetching
5. adjective
6. b. Touchy K's griping about the puzzle created a commotion.

Page 12

1. longueur
2. logy
3. languor
4. lolled
5. adjective
6. a. Groggy L slouched with listlessness during the book's longsome parts.

1. litany
2. lachrymose
3. lamented
4. larceny
5. noun
6. d. A tearful L bewailed the elongated list of losses from the robbery.

Page 13

1. malingering
2. malady
3. mendacious
4. manifested
5. verb
6. a. Duplicitous M's disease materialized after he fabricated a disorder to dodge his tasks.

1. magistrate
2. manacles
3. Machiavellian
4. mulcting
5. noun
6. c. The bailiff placed devious M in fetters for his defrauding.

Page 14

1. necessitated
2. nugatory
3. nimiety
4. narcissism
5. verb
6. c. N's egotism warranted a superfluous amount of trivial things.

1. nimble
2. nemesis
3. noxious
4. nescient
5. adjective
6. c. N was oblivious of her apt opponent's pernicious ways.

© 2017 The Critical Thinking Co.™ • www.CriticalThinking.com • 800-458-4849

Page 15

1. oppugned
2. opprobrious
3. odious
4. oubliette
5. adjective
6. b. No one protested when disreputable O was imprisoned for his repugnant behavior.

1. obviated
2. onerous
3. otiose
4. obstinately
5. adverb
6. d. Indolent O tenaciously averted every oppressive task.

Page 16

1. palliating
2. palatable
3. pacifying
4. palisade
5. verb
6. c. The stockade was a copacetic solution for abating threats and allaying P.

1. peccant
2. penchant
3. perfidy
4. pilfering
5. noun
6. b. Erring P's inclinations for lifting were an infidelity.

Page 17

1. query
2. quagmire
3. quell
4. qualms
5. adverb
6. b. Q's inquiry into the impasse did little to repress her reluctance.

1. quibbling
2. quarrel
3. querulous
4. quietus
5. adjective
6. b. Crabby Q needed a release to stop carping after the clash.

Page 18

1. reprehensible
2. rankled
3. rancor
4. rife
5. adjective
6. b. Teeming with hostility, R's culpable behavior incensed the town.

1. recalcitrance
2. renounced
3. repugnant
4. recidivated
5. verb
6. d. R relinquished his contumacy but soon reverted back to his repulsive ways.

Page 19

1. salubriousness
2. salient
3. senescent
4. sallowness
5. noun
6. d. Elderly S had a notable jaundice and a lack of hardiness.

1. solicitously
2. scoffed
3. spurious
4. sortilege
5. adverb
6. c. S apprehensively derided the false charge of wizardry.

Page 20

1. tirades
2. traduce
3. temerity
4. tumultuous
5. adjective
6. b. T's gall led him to defame others in frenzied diatribes.

1. trouncing
2. torpid
3. timorous
4. tumid
5. noun
6. a. After the drubbing, a puffed and skittish T was feeling sluggish.

Page 21

1. uncouthness
2. unfettered
3. urbane
4. unregenerate
5. adjective
6. b. Unconstrained by refined behavior, unrepentant U continued her coarseness.

1. unflappable
2. upheaval
3. unerring
4. unprecedented
5. adjective
6. b. U remained levelheaded and impeccable during the unmatched pandemonium.

Page 22

1. voluptuary
2. vitiated
3. villatic
4. vestige
5. adjective
6. d. V was debased by indulgent pursuits and every remnant of his pastoral upbringing was gone.

1. velleity
2. vituperated
3. veracity
4. vociferously
5. adverb
6. a. V was shrilly assailed for her weak impulse for sincerity.

Page 23

1. wayfarer
2. whit
3. weary
4. waylaid
5. noun
6. b. The prostrate drifter didn't care one speck about being detained.

1. whetted
2. waywardness
3. wily
4. waggery
5. verb
6. a. The impishness aroused artful W's insubordination.

Page 24

1. Xanthippe
2. xenial
3. xenophobia
4. xanthous
5. adjective
6. d. Because of her nationalism, the blond shrew was not hospitable to X.

1. xenomania
2. xenodochium
3. xeric
4. xystus
5. adjective
6. d. X's fetish for foreign things led him to a hostel with a portico in an arid area.

Page 25

1. yokel
2. yearnings
3. yeasty
4. yammered
5. verb
6. a. Y, a bumpkin, blabbed about harebrained hankerings.

1. yeti
2. yawped
3. yielding
4. yonder
5. adverb
6. c. As the folklore creature appeared beyond the hill, a passive Y squawked.

Page 26

1. zappy
2. zenith
3. zest
4. zealot
5. noun
6. b. Z became buoyant when the ideologue's exuberance hit a climax.

1. zephyr
2. zipped
3. zanily
4. zeppelin
5. adverb
6. b. During the breath, Z daftly barreled onto the blimp.

© 2017 The Critical Thinking Co.™ • www.CriticalThinking.com • 800-458-4849

MW01618571

MATTEO TORCINOVICH

PUNKOUTURE

FASHIONING A REVOLT
1976 - 1986

GINGKO PRESS

PVC MOTORBIKE JACKET
In shiny black, pink or snakeskin
Sizes: 30" to 44" chest/bust **£9.90** + 60p P&P

FAST DELIVERY
P.V.C. STRAIGHTS
In shiny black, pink or snakeskin
Mens sizes: 26" to 38" waist. Girls sizes: size 8 (32" hips) to size 20 (44" hips) **£6.90** + 60p P&P

ALSO AVAILABLE
DRILL STRAIGHTS IN KHAKI, GREY OR GREEN
Mens sizes: 26" to 38" waist. Girls sizes: size 8 (32" hips) to size 20 (44" hips) **£5.90** + 60p P&P

PEG LEG TROUSERS
In a choice of 3 colours: grey, green and khaki. Mens sizes: 26" to 38" waist. Girls sizes: size 8 (32" hips) to size 20 (44" hips) **£5.90** + 60p P&P

CORD STRAIGHTS
(Similar to famous name makes)
in Navy or Brown
£5.90 + 60p P&P
Also in DENIM
Mens Sizes 26" to 40" Waist
Girls Sizes Size 8 (32" hip) To Size 22 (46" hip)

Send cheques, postal orders or cash to
MAINLINE(S)
51 Two Mile Hill Road, Kingswood, Bristol.
Callers welcome Fridays and Saturdays only

ALL AVAILABLE EXCLUSIVELY FROM ·PHAZE· DEPARTMENT (N) 44-46 HIGH BRIDGE, NEWCASTLE-UPON-TYNE, NE1 6BX. TEL: (0632) 616065

CHEQUES OR POSTAL ORDERS PAYABLE TO PHAZE: ADD 95p TO ORDERS UP TO £15 ADD £1·50 TO ORDERS OF GREATER VALUE: FOR OVERSEAS ADD 30% OF VALUE

DELIVERY 7-21 DAYS... NO CASH IN POST PLEASE... REMEMBER TO STATE YOUR SIZE

ALTER

We are a leading N
fo
supplying H
Buy DIRECT from us
Send a large S.A.
Tshirts, jackets,

Phaze (Dept.N), 44/46

BONDAGE TROUSERS
T-SHIRTS
LEOPARD TROUSERS
POST-FREE!!

TARTAN BONDAGE TROUSERS Red, Yellow or Green complete with zips, 7 leg straps and bum-flap. Sizes Guys 26 28 30 32, Girls 8 10 12 14 — £17.95.
Also Plain Black Drill Bondage Trousers £17.45.
Leopard Trousers, Fur Fabric, Drain Pipes. For best look order smallest size you can. Guys sizes 24 26 28 30 32 34, Girls sizes 8 10 12 14 16 — £18.50.
Bondage T-Shirts, zips, strap, small or medium — £5.45.
Also Bondage Shirts — all medium — £9.50.

("Photos by Max")

T-Shirts, Siouxsie, Anarchy (Motif), Specials, God Save The Queen, small or medium, all £3.50.
Also Black/Red or Black/White.
Check T-Shirts, small or medium — £3.50.
Leopard-Print T-Shirts, Red or Yellow, small or medium — £3.50.

Please state second colour choice. Money cheerfully refunded if not completely satisfied.

Sorry, no Catalogues, only SAE enquiries replied. For Overseas Orders add 75p postage per item. Cheques/PO's to:

B. LEACH
50d (Basement)
REDCLIFFE GARDENS
CHELSEA, LONDON SW10

BLACK LEATHER

Jeans

Squeeze into **SLICK, TIGHT**-fitting, ankle length jeans, in **soft black hide**.
Sizes: 8-16. State waist, hip and inside leg to ankle.
Only **£37.25** inc p/p
Send cheque/P.O.
Satisfaction or refund
Credit Card Holders Send No. or Phone Leicester 530886 (office hours).

SHARON KIDSON (NME 46)
2 Hotel Street, Leicester LE1 5AW

punk leathers

SUPERBLY MADE LEATHER JACKETS MADE FROM SOFT HIDE SKINS, FULLY LINED AND MADE IN ENGLAND.

COLOURS BLACK AND BROWN
CHEST SIZES 36", 38", 40", 42", 44"

im fit jacket with pleated zip front, panelled ck and leather waistband - rings on chest am for pins, chains etc

39.95 EACH + 70p postage and packing

State clearly size and colour together with your name address and postal code. Send cheques, postal orders, Access/Barclaycard nos. to:

PUNK LEATHERS
31, CROSS CHEAPING
COVENTRY CV1 1HF

Please allow 10-14 days for delivery. Money back gaurantee if not fully satisfied if returned unworn within 7 days.

Double postage and packing outside UK.

ATHER
High Quality
ANUFACTURER
TTON JACKET.
ts and
P&P £1.50.
brown/black,
chest size 34-42

YCLE JACKET
ther. Two zip poc-
t and cuffs, adjust-

P&P £1.50.
Chest size
34 to 42
ng please state size
Send cash, cheque,
to:
Lionel Levy Ltd.,
hurst Road,
on E8 1JN.
days for delivery.

ETS MADE
LINED AND

th your name
postal orders,

y back gauran-
within 7 days.

Authentic looking
razor blades and
on high quality c
Cap sleeve.S.
£2.65 in

Send cheque/p.
size and quantity
O.K. PRINT
43 MELROS
BIRCH HILL
BRACKNELL

IRTS
ains,
s printed
on.
o&p
tating
ERKS.

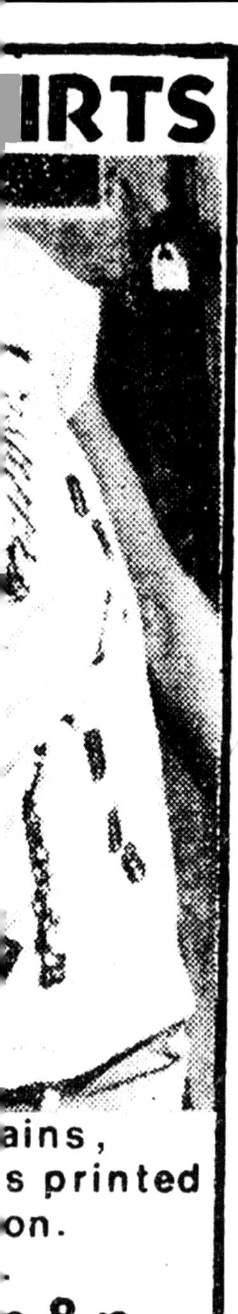

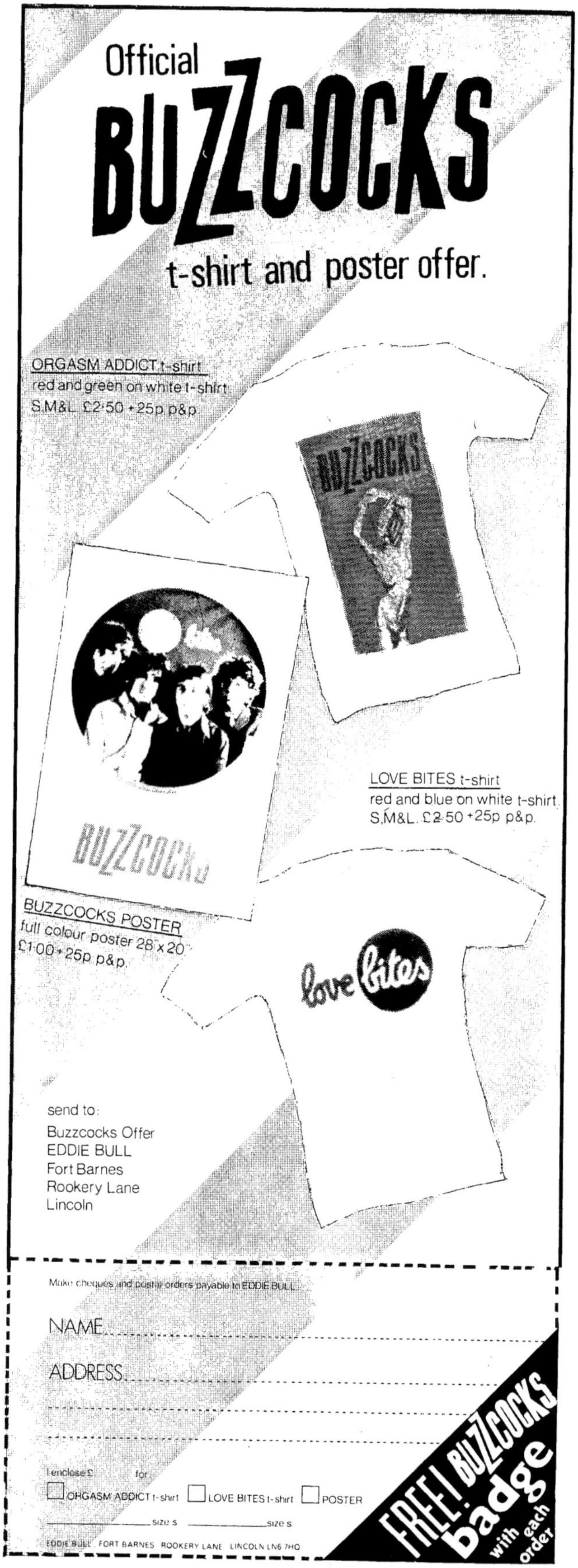
Official
BUZZCOCKS
t-shirt and poster offer.
ORGASM ADDICT t-shirt
red and green on white t-shirt
S.M&L. £2·50 +25p p&p.
BUZZCOCKS
LOVE BITES t-shirt
red and blue on white t-shirt
S,M&L. £2·50 +25p p&p.
BUZZCOCKS
BUZZCOCKS POSTER
full colour poster 28"x20"
£1·00+25p p&p.
love bites
send to:
Buzzcocks Offer
EDDIE BULL
Fort Barnes
Rookery Lane
Lincoln
Make cheques and postal orders payable to EDDIE BULL
NAME
ADDRESS
I enclose £ for
ORGASM ADDICT t-shirt
LOVE BITES t-shirt
POSTER
size s
size s
EDDIE BULL . FORT BARNES . ROOKERY LANE . LINCOLN LN6 7HQ
FREE! BUZZCOCKS badge with each order

YOUR PALS AT
MANIC P
WISH YOU
SEASONS CR
KOOL
KLOTHES
FOR A HAPPY
NEW WAVE
YEAR!
SNOOKY
MARIE

Amuse yourself in Wash & Wear Art.
no. 1002 3XL LONG: $14.00 ea.
Send check or mon
16075 La Monde
PHOTOGRAPHY: J. SKALICKY
no. 1021 SML: $13.00 ea.
Enfants Terrible
no. 1020 SML: $12.00 ea.
Tax &

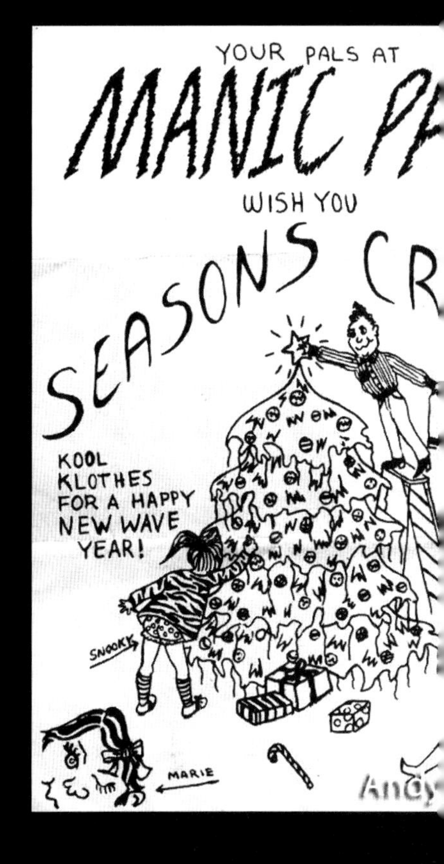

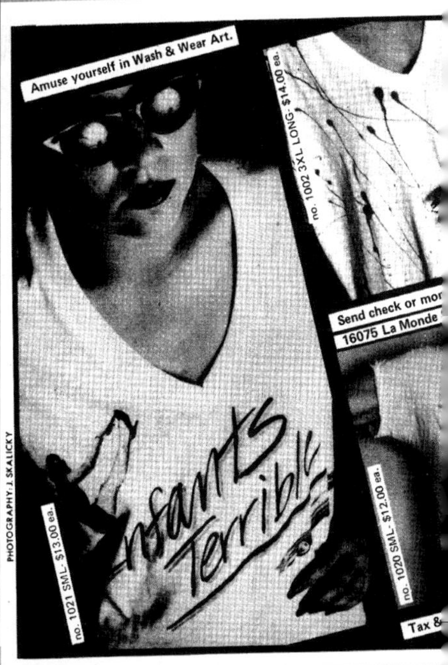

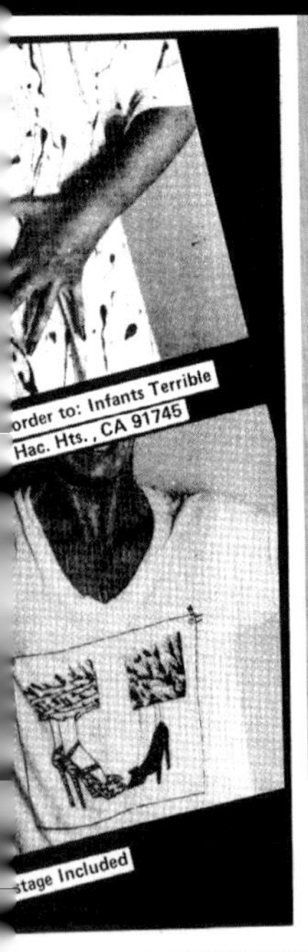

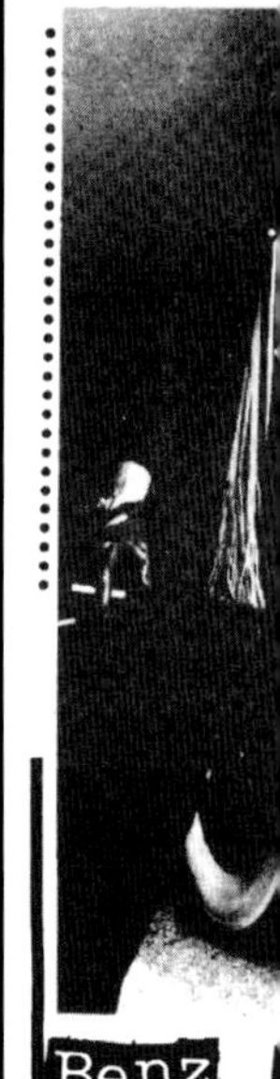

·153
SE
Long
Shir
fabr
clips
·As v
Pisto
follo
desig
Dest
God
1 per
·Deliv
·£9·25
·Wholes

S T I F F

With the following slogans:

IF IT AIN'T STIFF IT AIN'T WORTH A FUCK (black or white)

STIFF WORLD TOUR-1980 WE CAME WE SAW WE LEFT (Artist list on rear)

S H I R T S

In black, specify size, S-M-L.
Send check or money
STIFF TEES 157 West 57 Street,

'RY ANYTHING BUT
INCEST AND
FOLK DANCING

FUCK ART
LET'S DANCE

IT WORKS BETTER
IF YOU
PLUG IT IN

SEX & DRUGS &
ROCK & ROLL
(with STIFF logo)

00ea. 2for$13.00
er to:
w York,N.Y.10019

NEO80

CONSPICUOUS CLOTHING

7825 Melrose Avenue, Los Angeles 90046 213/852-9013

FOTO - KENT MARSHALL

469-8359

7^{00}

GRANNY'S of LONDON

sex pistols t-shirts...

new shipment in!

8953 Sunset Strip

Hollywood 550-9115

Dedicated to Countess Platessa Basinška Brancusi

PUNKO

UTURE

USER MANUAL: POLYSEXUALISM IN FASHION

DRESSING PUNK IS LIKE MAKING PUNK MUSIC: ANYONE CAN TAKE AN INSTRUMENT IN HAND, START PLAYING, MAKE UP A SONG, OR CONCOCT A LOOK THAT'S STUNNING WITH WHATEVER IS AROUND.

A young Malcolm McLaren also recognized that music and fashion were two sides of the same coin. In 1971, he renamed his Chelsea boutique "Let It Rock," and began selling records, memorabilia, and second-hand clothes, as well as new creations designed by his girlfriend, Vivienne Westwood.

The semiotics of punk and fashion had a common thread of deliberate agitation and sexual provocation, although this language resonated with diverse accents: sociopolitical themes were stressed in London; shabby street-style was popular in New York, and Los Angeles punk drew from the glamour of Hollywood.

This style affirmed its new identity and freed people to personalize their images using everyday items: bits and bobs found in the back of drawers, and attics; black leather jackets, fishnet stockings and stilettos worn with micro-mini skirts, cut-up and adapted garments; faded, slashed and frayed jeans; shiny black trousers and boots; and embellished T-shirts and tattered tops. S&M or bondage accessories were popular, along with chastity belts, straitjackets, handcuffs, chains, dogcollars, and other leather straps around arms, shoulders, legs and ankles — often finished off with the requisite black leather peaked cap.

Otherwise, second-hand garb from the fifties dominated, with an acidic injection of the psychedelic sixties. The darkest wrap-around shades were deemed de rigueur… the eyes never to be glimpsed.

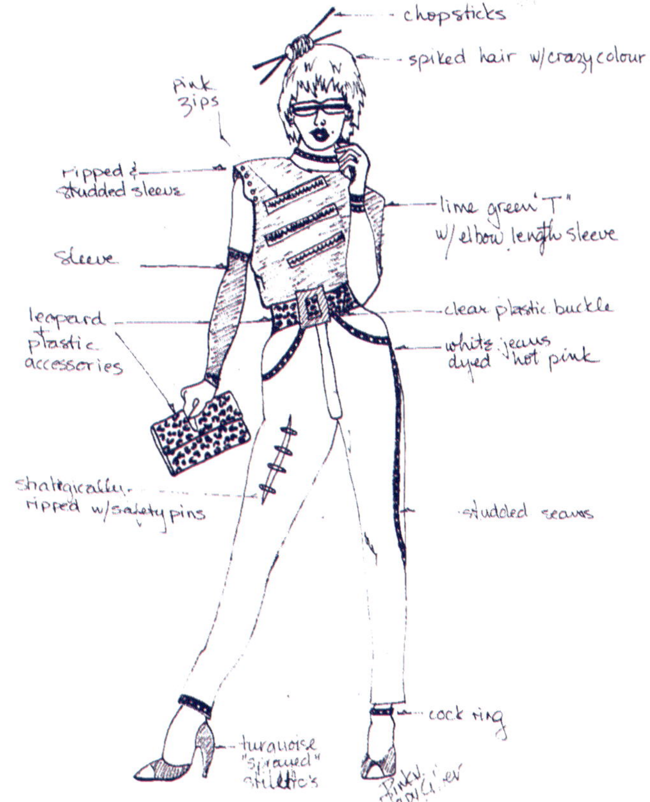

1981, New York
Lizzy Mercier Descloux
Photo Edo Bertoglio

10 - 11/1979, "Shades" #7
(Canadian fanzine)

Clothes were decorated in an individualist style, including stenciled slogans, silk-screen, and decadent animal prints. The lingerie-look also worked well. Punk is "polysexualism in fashion": for men, women, transsexuals, the androgynous.

Costume jewelry was a treasure trove of adornments to indulge in: safety pins, staples and clothes pegs, old badges, buttons, pendants, military medals, toilet chains, dog leashes, padlocks, bottle openers, cordage of various measures, studs, nuts and bolts, washers, toy guns, razor blades, pocket knives and plastic daggers, even old ties and broken bits of shoe… all tied, pinned, clipped, stapled, or glued to clothes.

Asymmetry was essential to achieving a certain drama in appearance. The two sides of the body were rarely bedecked in the same manner. It was not unusual to sport a black lace sock on one leg and a striped one on the other. This applied to makeup too: left and right sides of the face were to be marked in different ways. There weren't any rules or predefined styles for hair dye just yet.

Decidedly glamorous outfits emerged through the clever combination of various elements — though, in another context, they might have seemed exaggeratedly kitsch. In any case, punk urged self-expression, without censorship nor sacrosanct rules.

1979, New York
Tomata Du Plenty
Photo Edo Bertoglio

Nos 1-20
MORE STALLS
Cafe
REZILLOS
MAN in THE MOON

PUNKOUTURE
IS A GUIDE DIVIDED INTO SIX SECTIONS:
CLOTHES, HAIRSTYLE, MAKEUP, FOOTWEAR,
ACCESSORIES, AND SHOPPING.

A THREAD RUNS THROUGH ALL THAT
HAS BEEN FASHIONED INTO PUNK.
THIS GUIDE TRACES AND RESTITCHES
IT TOGETHER.

1977, London
Jerry Nolan, Heartbreakers
Photo Masayoshi Sukita

CLOTHES

COLORIZE, CUT, RIP TO SHREDS, RE-AFFIX

JORDAN
ADAM AND THE ANTS
MARQUEE CLUB
SIMON BARKER AKA SIX
JOHNNY ROTTEN
MARLIZ
PATTI PALLADIN
KEEF PAUL
PETER GRAVELLE
JUDY BALLANTINE
GLENDA MCNEIL
JEROME HIGGINS
BEN OR
SUBWAY NEWS
DR. RICHARD WALLACE
MEREDITH JACOBSON MARCIANO

1976 BRAVO

SEX PISTOLS
POP
CLAUDIA SKODA
ESTHER FRIEDMAN

1977 SORRISI E CANZONI

THERESE ANN SAVOY
DISCHI RICORDI
NUOVO SOUND

1978 YUGOSLAVIA

DZUBOKS

DIY!

3D TEES
HUBBA HUBBA
HIGH SOCIETY
FIORUCCI
SACHA
TAKE IT!
PSYCLONE
THE ADVERTS
HARRY T. MURLOWSKY
IGOR MOUKHIN
MASAYOSHI SUKITA
DEBBIE HARRY
PUNK
CREEM

ANTI-FASHION

JOHNNY THUNDERS
PETER GRAVELLE
THE OBSERVER
GENERATION X
CHRYSALIS RECORDS

PRINTED MATTER

SNIFFIN' GLUE
MARK PERRY
TERRY JONES
ISABELLE ANSCOMBE
NOT ANOTHER PUNK BOOK
I-D
STIFF RECORDS
CHRIS MORTON
NEVILLE BRODY
HAMISH ORR
EDDIE KING
BARNEY BUBBLES
ILLEGAL RECORDS
NEW HORMONES
RAW
ROUGH TRADE
JAMIE REID
MALCOLM GARRETT
PETER SAVILLE
RUSSELL MILLS
AURUM PRESS
THE DAILY MAIL
COUM TRANSMISSION
NICHOLAS FAIBAIRN
PROSTITUTION
ICA
GENESIS P-ORRIDGE
BOY
SIMON BARKER
VIVIENNE WESTWOOD
SEDITIONARIES
DEBBIE JUVENILE AKA LITTLE DEBBS
BROMLEY CONTINGENT
SEX PISTOLS
GLEN MATLOCK
PAUL COOK
PINK FLOYD
STEVE JONES
JOHNNY ROTTEN
BRAVO
ACME ATTRACTIONS
BOY
KITSCH-22
ZANDRA RHODES
CONCEPTUAL CHIC
ALTERNATIVE CLOTHES SHOW
CHELSEA TOWN HALL
INDIVIDUAL CLOTHES SHOW
HEAVEN
CAMDEN PALACE
THE LONDON FASHION SHOW
YVONNE GOLD
LEONARD
ROBYN BEECHE
NEW YORK ROCKER
PSYCLONE
NOMAG
BRUCE KALBERG
EWA WOJCIAK

NOMAG SAN FRANCISCO

SUSANNA HOFFS
BELINDA CARLISLE
GERMS
GEZA X
BRIAN GREGORY
CRAMPS
THE MENTORS
EL DUCE
LOUISE SPENCER
LINDA MODERN
NERVOUS GENDER
MICHAEL & GIRALDO
TEXACALA JONES
TEX AND THE HORSEHEAD
MS. PINKIE

WET LOS ANGELES

LEONARD KOREN
ED RUSCHA
COCA-COLA
PET ROCKS

DAMAGE LOS ANGELES

WESTERN FRONT FESTIVAL
SOCIETY FOR MANDATORY MODERN
SHELLAGH HANNIGAN
STEPHANO PAOLILLO
A. MARSH
GENETIC DAMAGE
BEVAN
BIOHAZARD
TERMINAL VELOCITY
SAAND
WES BOND
DANIEL GRIMES
FUSION
HANK FORD
DEL RAY
SONY SKATES
CARL WOLF
FLAMABLE KITCHEN FASHIONS
RAY GUN (NICK'URBANIAK)
SAXON
GARY MILES
BARBARA WHITE
SUSAN FRIEDMAN
JAPANESE WEEKEND
BAZOOKA JOE
CAROL ALTER
SUPPLIES
STACATTO DYSDAIN (A.K.A
JEORGIA A.)
LUTHER BLUE
NEW YORK - COMES - TO - NORTH
BEACH

FILE TORONTO

GENERAL IDEA
MAIL ART

SHADES TORONTO

GEORGE HIGTON
LELA MICHAEL
LEIGHTON BARRETT
EXCEL
BIM-BAM TUNNEL
MARGHERITA PASSION
NEW ROSE
JOHNNY ROTTEN
ALGICYRUSS
STEVE RASMUSSEN
ANDRÉE GAGNÉ
GERALD FRANKLIN
AMELIA EARHART
RAINBOW ROOM

A BUMPER COMMERCIAL BOOM

SMASH HITS
GRINGO CASUALS CO.
SOUNDS
NEW MUSICAL EXPRESS
RECORD MIRROR
CLASH
ADAM ANT
ENERGY DOME
DEVO
BETTER BADGES
JOLY MACFIE
FESTIVAL MONT DE MARSAN
JAMMING FANZINE
NO CURE FANZINE
PANACHE FANZINE
FUCK OFF RECORDS
PAOLA QUERIN

FIORUCCI NIGHTMARE

ETTORE SOTTSASS
STUDIO 54
GREGORY POE
MEREDITH JACOBSON MARCIANO
STUFF
CARLA WEBER
ROBERTO ROCCHI
ELVIS PRESLEY
PORTIERE DI NOTTE
NUOVO SOUND
LOREDANA SOTTILE
PLAYMEN
THE TEEN IDLES

PERESTROIKA WAVE

NAUTILUS POMPILUS
SVERDLOVSK
IGOR MOUKHIN
ROXY CLUB
DR MARTENS
VOENTORG
TUPIE
NATASHA
DUNYA SMIRNOVA
OLEG GARKUSHA
ZOMBIE
SAMIZDAT
MAGNETI
RALPH GIBSON
EDO BERTOGLIO
JIMMY JOCOY

THIS DOO
SSING
DRESSING
E IS A
THE
THE

1977-1978, London
Jordan and the Ants kids
Adam and the Ants gig
Back stage dressing room
The Marquee Club
Photo Simon Barker (aka SIX)

COLORIZE, CUT, RIP TO SHREDS, RE-AFFIX

"...WE WANT TO SWEEP AWAY THE WHOLE ROCK SCENE. WE HATE EVERYTHING THAT IS NICE, MIDDLE-CLASS AND BORING..."

Johnny Rotten

Punk was a brutal affront to the swanky bourgeoisie, simply achieved by donning ugly garments and combining them in the most absurd way:

• Prison-issue slacks with a weightlifter's belt and leather braces;
• Straitjackets with chains, belts, and buckles in abundance;
• Trousers fashioned out of bin-liners;
• All manner of leather or PVC trousers;
• Gashed fishnet stockings;
• Threadbare skirts held together with huge safetypins and duct tape.

Between 1976 and 1978, printed lists of clothes and accessories like this one could be gleaned from various journals worldwide: teenage weeklies, the music press, fashion supplements, tabloids and broadsheets, even porn magazines. To be a punk was to be scandalous, scabrous, censurable, and censored. Intriguing yet impenetrable to outsiders, this weird movement started making news.

In Los Angeles, 1977, a certain Marliz produced *Punk Rock – The New Wave of Sound & Style – How To Look Punk*. It was a fanzine-style manual containing various features that carefully explained how to be or become a real punk, from how to dance the pogo to how to wear chains with padlocks. Readers learned how to combine chains with ties, cords, and safety pins; how to cut a T-shirt properly; how to apply makeup or cut your hair. All info was accompanied by explanatory photos that showed what to do in detailed steps.

Newspapers attributed evermore meanings to the word "punk," so it became synonymous with unpleasant epithets: dirty, sordid, slutty, stinky, disgusting, deviant, odious, senseless, intoxicated, ugly, nasty, miserable, mean, petty.

In turn, those identifying as punks espoused some of these descriptors proudly. "The uglier, the punkier" become their watchword. "My clothes come out of the dustbin," stated Johnny Rotten. "It all depends on what you make them into."

1977, London
Elgin Mews North,
Maida Vale
Patti Palladin and Keef Paul
Photo Peter Gravelle

1977, "Punk Rock"
How to look punk
by Marliz
(US fanzine)

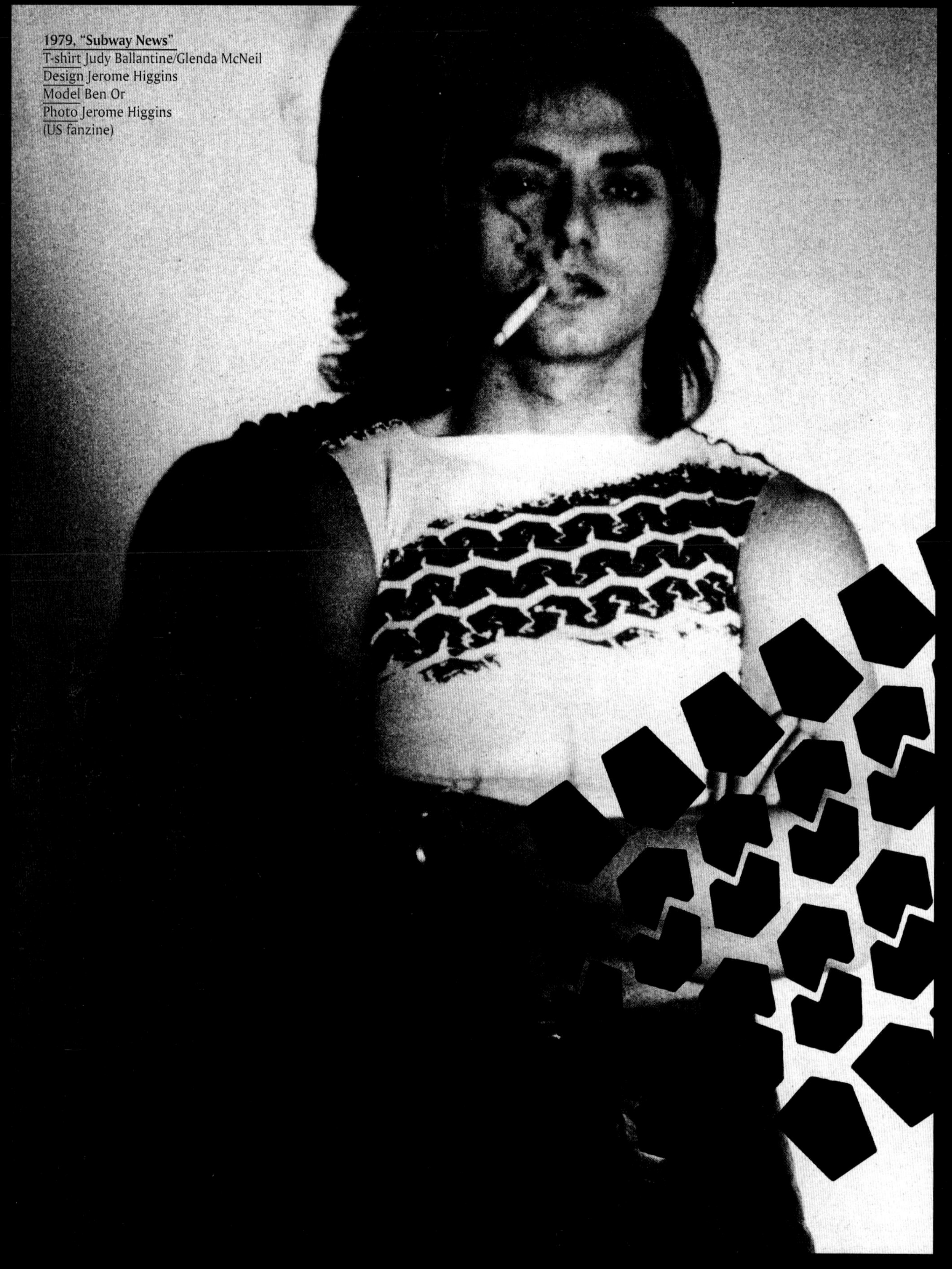

1979, "Subway News"
T-shirt Judy Ballantine/Glenda McNeil
Design Jerome Higgins
Model Ben Or
Photo Jerome Higgins
(US fanzine)

"This is Richard [Dr. Richard Wallace], who I met in '79.
He saw me in my Poseur's 'The Jam' shirt in the market near school and followed me. There were so few people into punk at University of Southern California at that time, [so] we had to find each other.
I had him star in a film I made where he's alienated and jumps off the HOLLYWOOD sign. We climbed up there. He was very bright; later he built the first robot A.L.I.C.E."

Photo Meredith Jacobson Marciano

1976
BRAVO

11.1977, "Pop" (West German magazine)

In September 1976, Bravo, the German teen magazine, titled an article: "Fashion tips for crazy parties - PUNK FOR FUN AND FREAKING OUT."

"For a punk face: straight hair combed back (with hair cream or sugar and water), with locks hanging over the face; dark sunglasses, possibly broken; heavily made-up eyebrows, cheeks and lips.

For a Sex Pistols style: unisex looks, jeans with countless safety pins, striped socks and old sneakers. Over military vests, the latest craze, a thinly knotted tie is worn with a white shirt decorated with pins, photos, and junk of all kinds attached with safety pins. An insanity: T-shirts and tank tops are painted or cut with zigzag scissors. Girls wear tight drain-pipe jeans, very high-cut shorts (put an elastic band on trousers hems and decorate them with lots of zips) or loose-fitting trousers made of plastic tablecloths. For boys: skin-tight black pants.

Black, the punk fashion color! For boys: cut shirt sleeves with scissors; paint barbed wire using fabric colorant. It takes a studded belt and chain bracelets. For girls: fishnet stockings and high-heeled shoes; clown makeup and ruffled carnival wigs.

Go totally crazy with colored hair: comb your hair back and spray it according to your fancy with colored hair spray; exaggerate eyes and eyebrows with black liner.

Shocking prank: push the head of a clipped-off safety pin into the cheek, it will look like it's stuck in!

Punk kittens have sharp claws: buy fake nails and stick them on top of your own, painting them first with red and then black.

The real punk freaks have disheveled hair, ashenwhite faces, black shades hiding the eyes, lilac lips. T-shirts with cigarette burns are all the rage.

As jewelry: an old bog chain around the throat!"

BRAVO-Modetip für irre Partys

PUNK ZUM SPASS UND AUSFLIPPEN

02-1978, "Bravo" (West German Magazine)

11.1977, "Pop" (West German Magazine)

PUNK-MODE
von der
Müllkippe
PUNK
ROC
UNK

B-AV5408
B-NR706

1979, West Berlin
Zossener Straße, Claudia & Rosi
Clothes Claudia Skoda
Photo Esther Friedman

DEUTSCHE REICHSBAHN
WESTKREUZ
DEUTSCHE REICHSBAHN
Westkreuz

1979, West Berlin
S-Bahn Westkreuz
Rosalia & Friends, 1978, Streetwear
Photo Esther Friedman

1977 SORRISI E CANZONI

In 1977, a major Italian TV guide, *Sorrisi e Canzoni*, elucidated as follows: "The aim is to horrify others in dress and hairstyle. This is why 'punks' go around in tatters; they dye their hair three or four different colors; they stick safety pins into their cheeks (there's a spot that is fairly insensitive — it's like wearing an earring); they don't wash, and their language is the most violent possible. Born as a movement based on attitude (rejection of society) and music ('punk-rock' numbers dozens of bands), punk was soon exploited from an economic point of view. Stores have sprung up specializing in 'punk' attire, where even plastic hands and feet that ooze fake blood are sold, as well as collars that 'punk' women love to have their men put around their necks. There are imitators even in Italy. But their mode of being 'punk' only goes as far as clothes."

1978 DISCHI RICORDI DISTRIBUTION

In 1978, *Dischi Ricordi* was the main Italian distributor for a smattering of punk rock records.

In order to enhance its wares, it promoted free plastic vests, which were fabricated from black garbage bags! To get your hands on this authentic punk tank-top, all you had to do was purchase one of their LPs...

11.1977, "TV Sorrisi e Canzoni"
Therese Ann Savoy presents punk fashion to her readers (Italian TV Guide)

01.1978, "Nuovo Sound"
Dischi Ricordi advert (Italian magazine)

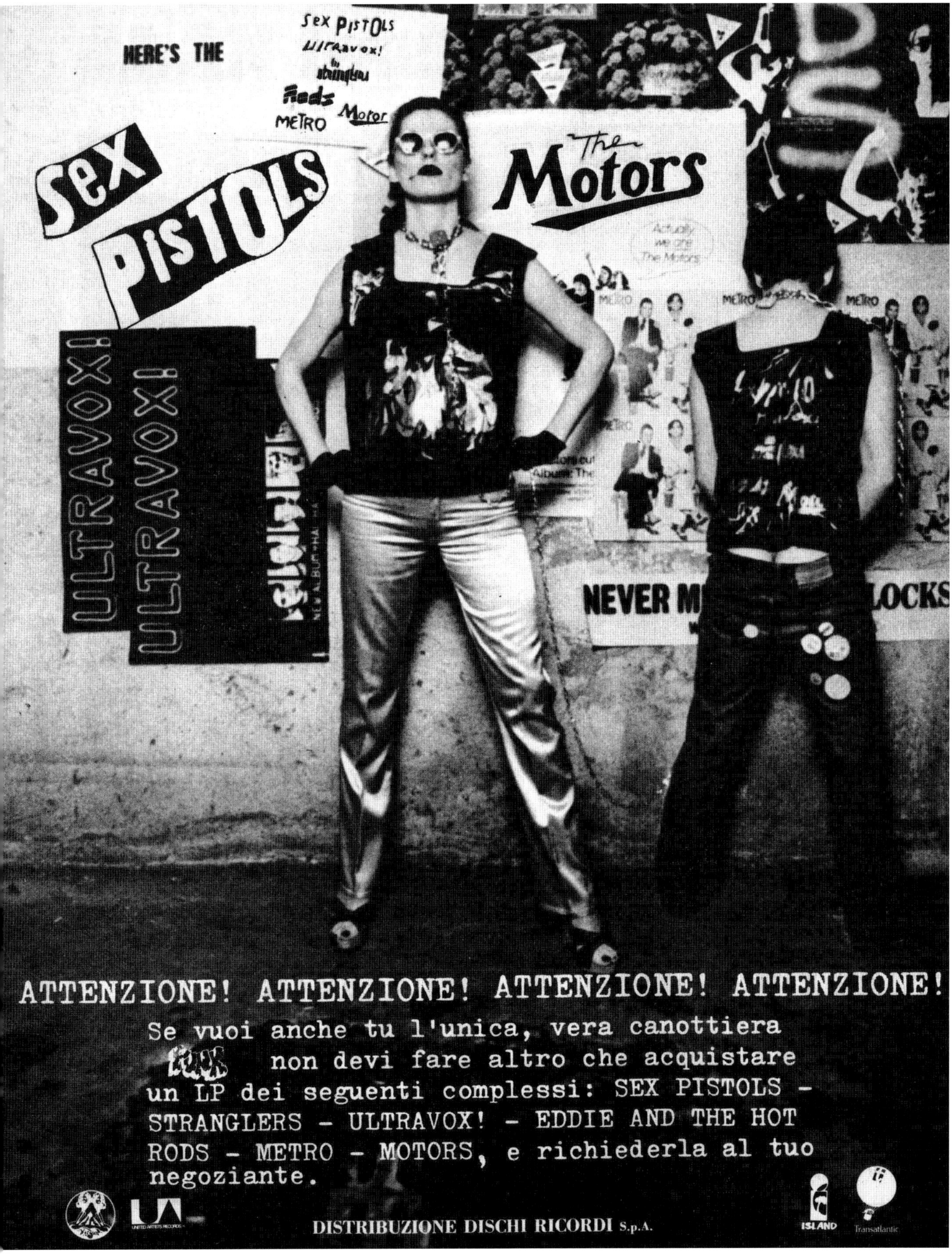

ATTENZIONE! ATTENZIONE! ATTENZIONE! ATTENZIONE!

Se vuoi anche tu l'unica, vera canottiera PUNK non devi fare altro che acquistare un LP dei seguenti complessi: SEX PISTOLS - STRANGLERS - ULTRAVOX! - EDDIE AND THE HOT RODS - METRO - MOTORS, e richiederla al tuo negoziante.

DISTRIBUZIONE DISCHI RICORDI S.p.A.

ISLAND Transatlantic

1978 YUGOSLAVIA

In Yugoslavia, a 1978 article entitled "Punk Moda" was included in the November edition of *Džuboks*:

"The pants are tight [...] A alternative is baggy pants tied at the ankles with laces.

Designs have no limitations [...] the more disgusting, the better: large flowers (no small flowers), stripes, and images of all sizes. The shirts have very small collars and are eccentrically decorated. The thin tie is mandatory for both sexes, or the simple T-shirts worn with a classic men's suit, two or three sizes too big, or with a leather jacket, probably black with zippers and as many studs as possible. Full-length working attire also works like mechanics' overalls, with lots of zips. Hairstyles: very short hair for both sexes, or, if kept longer, disheveled with some spikiness, dyed different colors.

Shocking makeup is not only for women. You shouldn't smile! If possible, pose in front of a large-cc motorbike with gloves and boots."

11.1978, "Džuboks"
(Yugoslavian magazine)

diki tisk
GROSUPLJE pp 3
PUNK
DISCO
NOVI SVETSKI MODNI HITOVI I KOD NAS!
CRVENA ILI CRNA ŽENSKA HALJINA SA PRESLIKAČEM PO ŽELJI
Cena 500 dinara
NOVE MAJICE DUGIH RUKAVA SA DVA LICA
Cena 300 dinara
Detaljnije informacije u Džuboksu

SILKSCREENED
FABRIC

Pauvette
415
7635116

FASHION

06.1977, "Psyclone"
(US fanzine)

>
1981, "Take It!"
3D Tees
On Sale Hubba Hubba, High Society, Fiorucci, Sacha Boston
(US fanzine)

DO IT YOURSELF!

WHEN THE WORD "PUNK" IS HITCHED TO FASHION IT INSTANTLY DELIMITS PUNK'S ORIGINAL MEANING: PUNK AS WIDE-OPENNESS TO ALL CROSS-CULTURAL INTERFERENCE. "PUNK FASHION" PIGEONHOLES 'NO-STYLE' INTO JUST ANOTHER UNIFORM.

A gaudy or fluorescent T-shirt, torn in such a way as to reveal overt "artistic" openings, could be termed "punk chic" if worn over a black skin-tight top with long sleeves.

Slash an old T-shirt to pieces, then fasten the resulting snippets of fabric back together with safety pins. Lacerate the sleeves, snip away and reassemble a new neckline, cut an asymmetrical opening at the front, crop a vest into a waistcoat shape... then reassemble the ensemble by aligning the pins neatly, as if they were stitches.

Scrawl the word "PUNK" on the front of any old top, with either fabric colorant, nail polish, or ink. Then adorn the letters with safety pins, badges, studs, chains — and add a macabre tinge with splatters of bloody red.

Scribble slogans: "Be reasonable – demand the impossible," "I'm a lazy sod," "Destroy," "You're gonna wake up one morning and know what side of the bed you've been lying on!," "Chaos," "Never trust a hippie," "Only anarchists are pretty," or "Anarchy for the UK means freedom from rubber bullets."

"....THOROUGHBRED PUNKS EXPLOIT ANY PHENOMENON THAT IS DEEMED FASHIONABLE. IN TODAY'S WORLD, IN GLOBAL CULTURE, WITH THIS PERMANENT CONSUMERIST FEVER, IT IS HARD TO MAINTAIN ORIGINALITY AND INTEGRITY..."

11.1978, "Džuboks"

The Adverts
Photo Harry T. Murlowsky

1986, Mosca
Young alternative punk rockers
Photo Igor Moukhin

1977, London
Photo Masayoshi Sukita

NEW
HEARTS

12.1976, "Punk"
Punk T-Shirts
(US fanzine)

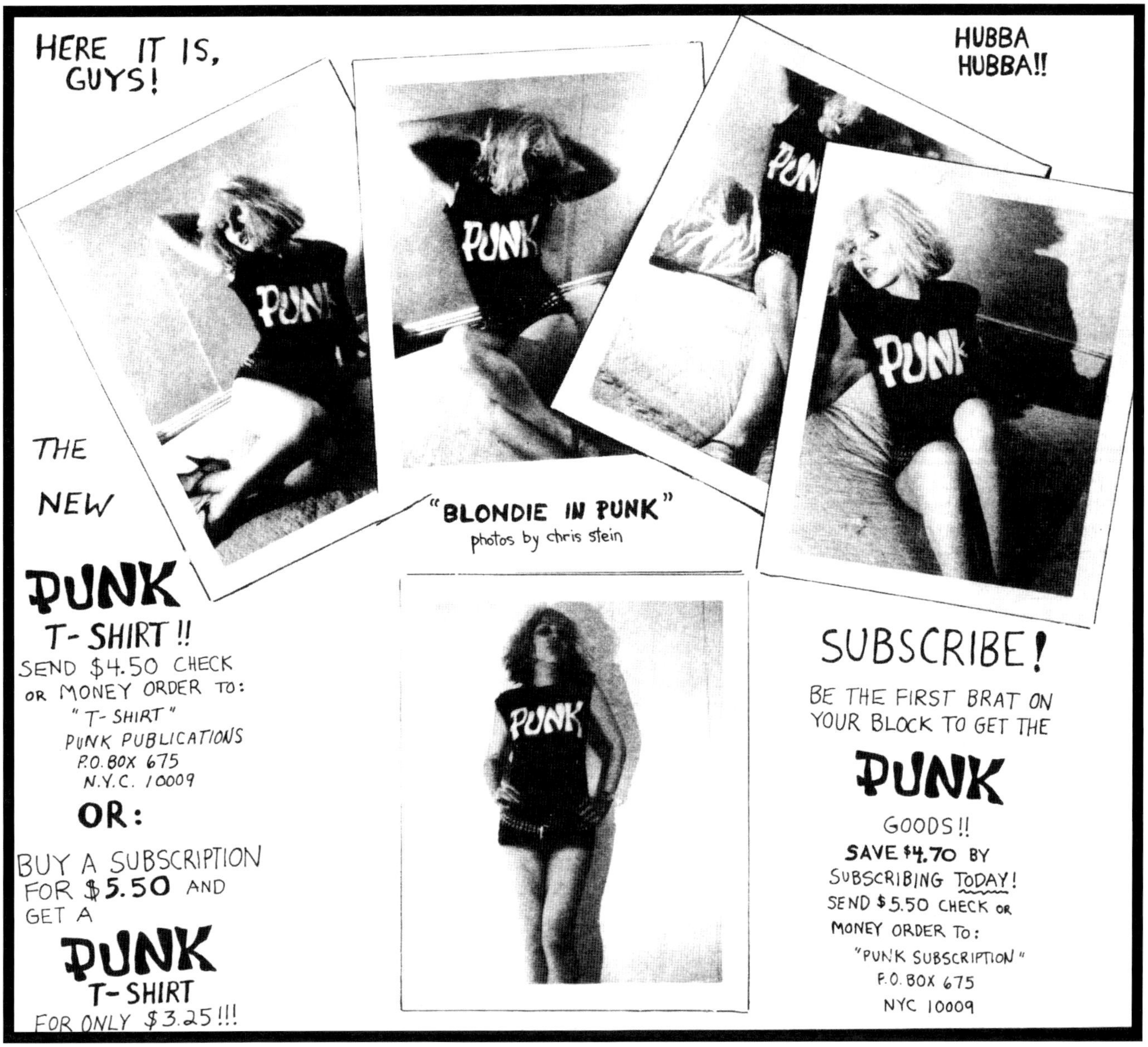

HERE IT IS, GUYS!
HUBBA HUBBA!!
PUNK
"BLONDIE IN PUNK"
photos by chris stein
THE NEW
PUNK
T-SHIRT !!
SEND $4.50 CHECK OR MONEY ORDER TO:
"T-SHIRT"
PUNK PUBLICATIONS
P.O. BOX 675
N.Y.C. 10009
OR:
BUY A SUBSCRIPTION FOR $5.50 AND GET A
PUNK
T-SHIRT
FOR ONLY $3.25!!!
SUBSCRIBE!
BE THE FIRST BRAT ON YOUR BLOCK TO GET THE
PUNK
GOODS!!
SAVE $4.70 BY SUBSCRIBING TODAY!
SEND $5.50 CHECK OR MONEY ORDER TO:
"PUNK SUBSCRIPTION"
P.O. BOX 675
NYC 10009

04.1976, "Punk"
Debbie Harry
Endoresement for "Punk" T-shirt
(US fanzine)

10.1977, "Creem"
T-shirt with PUNK razor blade
(US magazine)

03.1976, "Punk"
"Be a punk... wear a punk T-shirt!"
(US fanzine)

PUNKS!
CREATE YOUR OWN ANARCHY
PUNK
100% Cotton Black T-Shirt
Blade is Silk Screened with
Metallic Finish – Will not Fade or Peel.
NEXT WORLD
P.O. Box 693305
Miami, Fl. 33169
Allow 4 weeks for delivery.
Price $3.95 + .50 postage and handling per shirt.
Fl. residents add 4% sales tax.
Name
Address
City State Zip
Check Size
S M L
Zip Code must be included to process order.

BE A PUNK
WEAR A PUNK T-SHIRT!
PUNK
SEND $3.00 CHECK OR MONEY ORDER
TO PUNK T-SHIRT
356 10TH AVENUE
N.Y.C., N.Y. 10001
BLACK ON WHITE
WHITE ON BLACK
LARGE MEDIUM SMALL
NAME
ADDRESS
CITY STATE ZIP

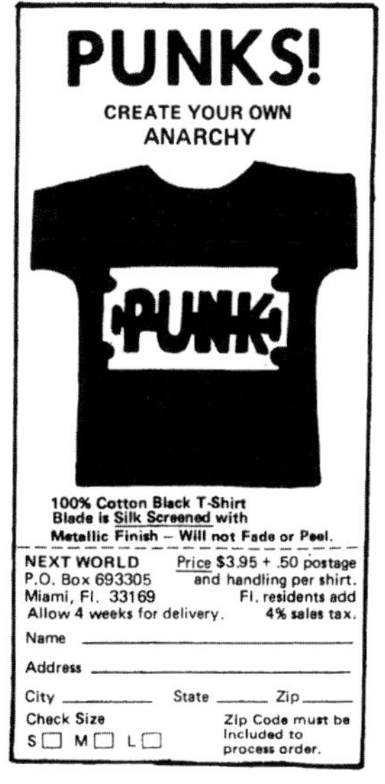

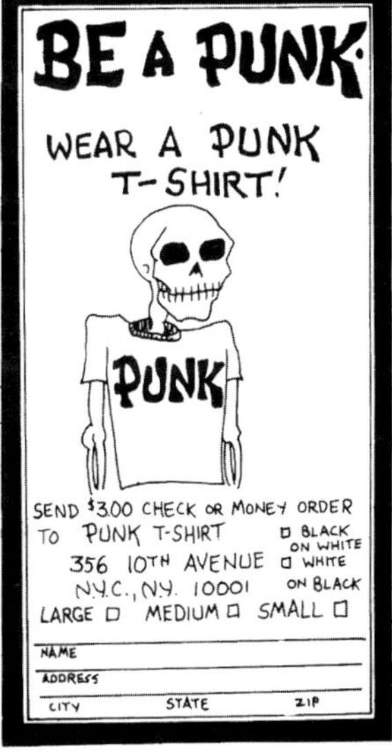

ANTI-FASHION

Despite the rules promulgated by the press, you didn't need anything or anyone in order to dress punk. No-thing: because you can wear absolutely anything, convention be damned. No-one: because nobody can to tell you what to wear or how to wear it. Above all, you don't need to purchase a single item from any shop.

An "anti-fashion" against fashion, against conventions, "punk" is a term closely related to the individualistic, self-sufficient attitude of do it yourself. However, as a youth movement, it also inevitably became form of a social, collective expression, involving conformity in appearance and behavior: it succumbed and turned into a fashion. Punk fashion…a perfect paradox!

In those years of boredom and cultural uniformity, this "pernicious approach" rapidly went viral, not only infecting teenagers but also piquing the interest of journalists and, shortly thereafter, the record industry — as well as the rag trade, which appreciated the phenomenon and reaped the most from its novelty. Punk went commercial. The new aesthetic took shape and spread like wildfire throughout the globe. From London to the USA, the mid-seventies heard the cry of new musical realities. Then complementary fashion outlets emerged everywhere — from Los Angeles to San Francisco, Boston to Philadelphia, Toronto and back to Europe — new stores and boutiques offered innovative fabrics, clothes, accessories, and merchandise of every ilk. But it was in Britain where the new style had the greatest impact, catalyzing a vast, irrepressible proliferation of fanzines, records, gigs, and artistic happenings.

1977, London, Chelsea
Johnny Thunders
Photo Peter Gravelle

01.1977, "The Observer"

1977, Generation X
The day they signed with
Chrysalis Records
Photo Peter Gravelle

PRINTED MATTER

The fanzine that set the standard was *Sniffin' Glue* by Mark Perry, for it was giddy with content — reviews, interviews, insider information — and a sincere visual punch. All a fanzine publisher, like Perry, needed was a typewriter, scissors, camera, and photocopier. This monthly started off by printing fifty copies per issue and reached a peak circulation of fifteen thousand. Its unpretentious approach to graphics heralded a new era in print media. In 1978, Terry Jones and Isabelle Anscombe jolted the publishing industry with *Not Another Punk Book*, the most creative text on punk imagery and one of the first accounts to demonstrate punk as a style, a fashion. Inside, unpublished photos brim with detail within a fanzine-type layout, never before seen in book form. The result is a genuine masterpiece. Moreover, Terry Jones is noteworthy for being one of the 1980 co-founders of *i-D* magazine, the bimonthly that would ascend the throne of stylistic authority, and reign for several years, emulated by numerous periodicals, including mainstream publications.

There was no shortage of novelty bubbling up on the recording side too, including a return to the 7-inch format with a proliferation by fledgling independent labels: Stiff Records was pivotal, thanks to art director Chris Morton and an extraordinary staff of creatives including Neville Brody, Hamish Orr, Eddie King, as well as the unparalleled Barney Bubbles. A slew of other self-financing labels, such as Illegal Records, New Hormones, and Raw, recorded, designed and distributed their releases. The scene's new bands differentiated themselves musically and stood out visually via an image, created ad hoc by graphic artists like Jamie Reid, Malcolm Garrett, Peter Saville, Russell Mills.

1978, "Not Another Punk Book"
Terry Jones & Isabelle Anscombe
Publisher Aurum Press

06.1977, "Sniffin' Glue" #10
(UK fanzine)

ily Mail, Tuesday, October 19, 1976

'These people are the wreckers of civilisation'

Nicholas Fairbairn . . . outraged.

Adults only art show angers an MP

By THOMSON PRENTICE

TORY MP Nicholas Fairbairn fought his way through Hell's Angels and young men with multi-coloured hair, lipstick and nail varnish last night — all in the caus of art.

But what he saw turned him blue with anger.

For the show was called 'Prostitution.' Among the 'art' was a cage of chains and images of sadism and masochism.

And the MP's critical appraisal was: 'It's a sickening outrage. Sadistic. Obscene. Evil.'

His conclusion: 'The Arts Council must be scrapped after this.'

The adults-only show is being staged for a week at the Institute of Contemporary Arts, which receives a grant of £90,000 from the council.

It is the work of ex-student Neil Megson, 26, who has changed his name by deed poll to Genesis P. Orridge. He has appeared in court on an obscenity charge.

Mr Fairbairn, QC and MP for Kinross and West Perthshire said he would demand an explanation in the Commons from Arts Minister Harold Lever.

'Public money is being wasted here to destroy the morality of our society. These people are the wreckers of civilisation. They want to advance decadence.

'I came here to look, and I am horrified,' said the MP.

Mr Orridge, wearing silver nail varnish and with his shoulder-length black hair held in place by a turquoise plastic hair slide, said: 'We are presenting information. Without people, information is dead. People give it life.

'We are out for a little fun, but I accept that some people may think we are mad,' he added.

Mr Ted Little, artistic director of the ICA, explained that he did not exercise artistic judgment. 'I see my job as giving artists exposure.

'The arts in this country are still dominated by middle-class attitudes. This has got to be broken down.'

Arts Council representatives were at the opening and Mr Little, asked what they had thought of it, smiled and said: 'They left early.'

Visitors . . . what today's connoisseur is wearin

Judges' decision soon

AN important legal decision affecting the sale of pornography in Britain will follow an appeal this week by two newsagents convicted of selling hard-core porn magazines. The judges' decision will cover the question: Can an expert say in evilence that porn can do some people good?

"Daily Mail"
19 October 1976

The moment had arrived for the "wreckers of civilisation," as Tory MP Nicholas Fairbairn dubbed the art collective COUM Transmission. He was incensed after having reconnoitered *Prostitution*, the controversial exhibition curated by Genesis P-Orridge at London's ICA for one week in October 1976. *Prostitution* was a provocative "Sexhibition" of objects that explored pornographic imagery bordering on the abhorrent, realized with typical British shock factor, intended to incite outrage and capture attention in a characteristically British manner. The same incendiary impulse, a year later, would be displayed on the street, in the near-by shop window of BOY vetrine di BOY.

**"I LOVED THE SEX SHOP MORE THAN SEDITIONARIES. IT HAD A UNIQUE ATMOSPHERE.
ONCE INSIDE YOU DIDN'T WANT TO LEAVE; A SINGLE VISIT TO THE SHOP COULD LAST FOR HOURS. THE MIX OF THE CLIENTELE WAS GLAMOROUS AND ECLECTIC: PROSTITUTES, NEWSREADERS, POP STARS, MODELS AND PERVERTS. UNFORTUNATELY THE SHOP WAS REMODELED INTO SEDITIONARIES BEFORE I TOOK ANY PHOTOS INSIDE."**

Simon Barker

Amongst this ferment of uninhibited expression, in the sphere of fashion surfaced the creations of Vivienne Westwood. In an interview, she acknowledged that, though her clothes were too expensive for most, her artifacts were also prototypes, available to anyone who was inspired to copy and recreate what she sold in the shop. Otherwise, her vestments were flogged to the "punk aristocracy" of the moment from her shop at 340 King's Road, London: Seditionaries.

1977/1978, London
Shop girl - Debbie Juvenile
(aka Little Debbs)
Seditionaries, Kings Road
Photo Simon Barker (aka Six)

Westwood's creations were worn by the Sex Pistols and The Bromley Contingent.

"Shock is the look: bassist Glen Matlock wears red velvet shoes and bespattered pants, drummer Paul Cook a torn T-shirt with the words "I hate Pink Floyd," guitarist Steve Jones flaunts red gaiters and a shirt hand-painted with oils, the singer Johnny Rotten sports pajama breeches and a slashed velvet jacket barely held together by safety pins…" (*Bravo* magazine, September 1976).

The four Pistols were used as living endorsements, establishing Seditionaries as a reference point for punks. The shop retailed expensive garments without intellectual copyright. Those who couldn't afford them were free to fashion them for themselves…

At the same time, new shops, such as Acme Attractions, BOY, and Kitsch-22, mushroomed around London. Furthermore, punk was infiltrating haute couture: the farsighted Zandra Rhodes daringly presented her Conceptual Chic show in 1977, including strategically holed pink and black jerseys with beaded safety pins, designed for the high-end fashion market.

From that point on, London would succeed as the fashion capital of the world. By 1983, collections were launched at the Alternative Clothes Show, at Chelsea Town Hall, or at the Individual Clothes Show. Clubs like Heaven beneath Charing Cross and the Camden Palace started to host catwalk shows, culminating in 1986 with the London Fashion Show, an event attracting over nine thousand spectators, many from across the Channel.

1981, Zandra Rhodes
Makeup Yvonne Gold
Hair Leonard
Photo Robyn Beeche

09.1976, "Bravo"
(West German magazine)

Uralte Bilder und Embleme werden aufs Hemd geklebt

Mit Farbe und Schere hat Schlagzeuger Paul Cook sein „Pink Floyd"-T-Shirt „verschönert"

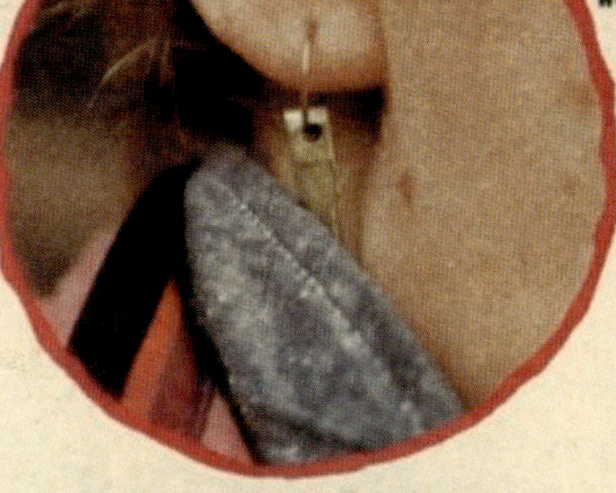

Ohrringe für Männer sind wieder der letzte Schrei, sie dürfen allerdings nicht wertvoll sein. Sänger Johnny Rotten trägt im Ohr ein Stück einfaches Blech

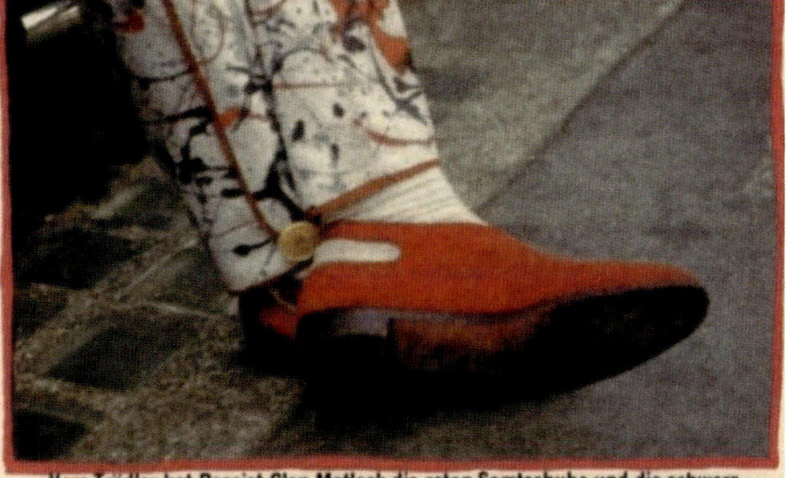

Vom Trödler hat Bassist Glen Matlock die roten Samtschuhe und die schwarz-weiß-rot gesprenkelte Hose

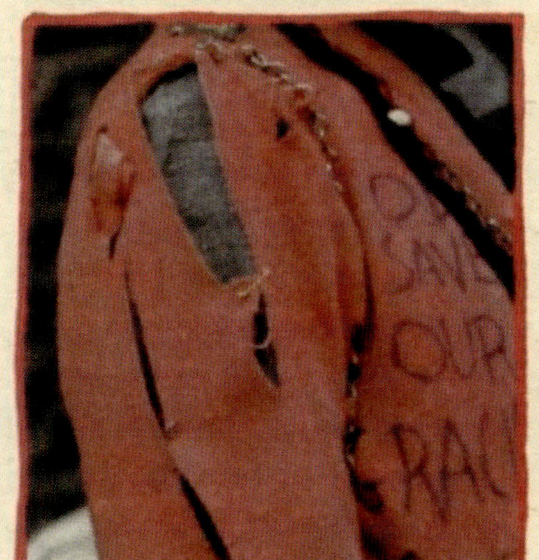

The tabloids generally ridiculed and often dismissed punk, highlighting furor and transgressions. Shock and outrage made the news. The tabloids summed up the King's Road as a meeting place for brainless grotesques and focused on Westwood's provocative swastikas or deranged kids dressed in garbage.

However, while most of the press treated the phenomena as little more than tittle-tattle, a passing youth fad or baffling joke, a few astute journalists had a more in-depth eye. Some serious editorials regarded punk as an appreciable artistic movement of sartorial statements and protest — much more than a mere freak show. It was in this vein, in New York, that *Punk,* the fanzine, emerged, followed by *New York Rocker*, and, over in San Francisco, the fanzines *Psyclone* and, importantly, NoMag, which was founded by Bruce Kalberg and his girlfriend Ewa Wojciak and published from 1978 to 1984.

03-04.1978, "WET"
WET T-Shirt, the perfect solution for any fashion problem
(US magazine)

NOMAG SAN FRANCISCO

NoMag ran for fourteen issues and contained highly original pages on fashion, detailing creative inventions and extravagant, provocative concoctions at the limit of wearability, alongside a visual assortment of sexual pathologies, medical atrocities, autopsies, dominatrixes at work, texts about female circumcision or tips on how to synthesize heroin from morphine, comicstrips, photos of used tampons, adverts for periodontal treatment… In addition, of course, pornography was included: Susanna Hoffs topless, Belinda Carlisle in pantyhose, Germs producer Geza X holding his dick, Brian Gregory of the Cramps semi-saluting his python, the irrepressible singer of The Mentors, El Duce, shitting on a plate… the chaos that Kalberg once called "the old cliché of shit-and-guts imagery," meant to wage war on polite society.

1980, "NoMag" #4
Louise Spencer
Model's restrictive hat & collar
Design Linda Modern for the passive woman

<
Michael & Giraldo
Suit with nails, plastic bubble wrap, studs and more
(US fanzine)

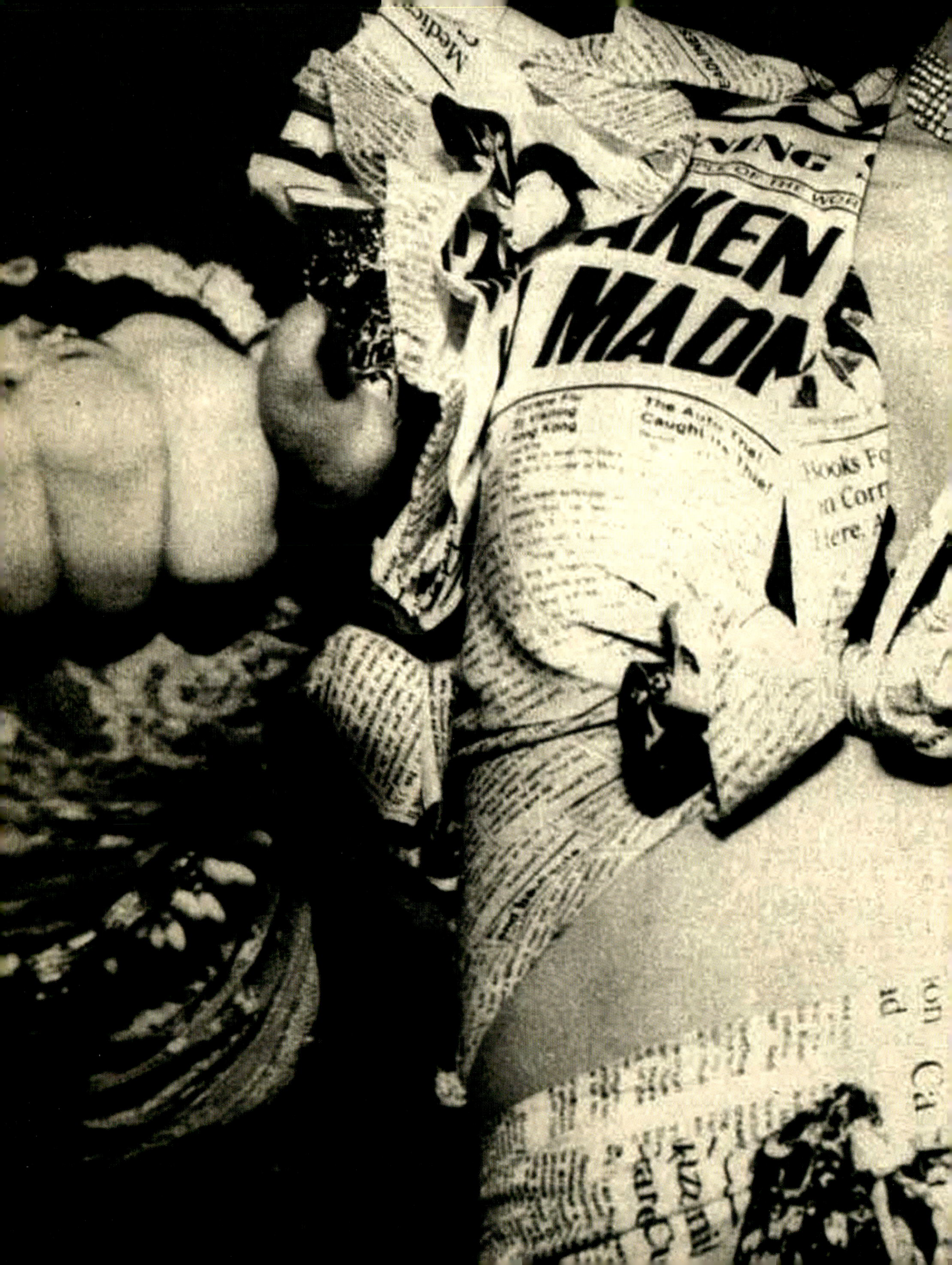

1984, "NoMag" # 13
Texacala Jones (Tex and the Horsehead)
Wearing News-Print Dress
Designed by Ms. Pinkie
(US fanzine)

Los Angeles gives birth to some notable fanzines: *Slash*, *Damage*, and *WET – The Magazine of Gourmet Bathing*.

WET LOS ANGELES

Thirty-four issues of *WET – The Magazine of Gourmet Bathing* were published by Leonard Koren between 1976 and 1981, noteworthy for their mix of so-called H_2O culture, light nudity, fashion, and wonderful ads for trendy Los Angeles boutiques.

WET - The Magazine of Gourmet Bathing's unusual mix of art, music, and clothes (from performance art to the work of Ed Ruscha) with innovative and influential graphics helped substantiate the specific New Wave aesthetic of LA.

In the first issue, Koren deliberates: "*WET* is a magazine devoted to upgrading the quality of your bathing experience. Hopefully, in the great American tradition of Coca-Cola, doggie diapers and Pet Rocks, *WET* will become one of the things you never imagined you needed until you find you can't live without it."

DAMAGE LOS ANGELES

The fanzine *Damage* notched up thirteen issues from July 1979 to June 1981, including a special freebie for the Western Front Festival (which it had co-sponsored). The fanzine used bold graphics and was full of photos, reviews and interviews of historical significance to the Californian punk scene. Number 3 (Oct. 1979) dedicates two pages to a curious fashion show, with a detailed article by Shellagh Hannigan and photos by Stephano Paolillo. The introductory text sets the stage:

"On August 30th at 8 p.m, the Society for Mandatory Modem Dress held its first fashion presentation. The Society is a visual artists' collective dedicated to providing an alternative for those opposed to buying mass-produced, high-priced clone clothing.

Filtering through the air at the sold-out Dovre Hall were various types of computed sound, music and personal/political/fashion statements.

Featuring fashions of the future for the present, each segment had its own theatrical high-lights:

Opening the show: Founder of the Society and her own Genetic Damage line, A. Marsh takes a scientific approach to fashion. Carrying lazer guns, her mannequins wore space suits with severely pointed shoulders and clinched-in waists…

01-02.1978, "WET"
The Magazine of Gourmet Bathing
(US magazine)

10.1979, "Damage" #3
(US fanzine)

S.F. FREE IN CALIFORNIA $1.00 ELSEWHERE L.A.

DAMAGE

OKTOBER

RIOT!

ON THE

WESTERN FRONT

These were made of grey primed canvas spraypainted, rip-stop nylon, and gold quilted nylon with matching arm and leg protectors. Each design represented a stage in a space voyage cycle.

A. Marsh believes, 'Artists must have control of technology to make sense of the future, to articulate the past.'

Which brings us to Bevan of Biohazard. While barraging the audience with pre-packaged fast food, her model patrolled the stage in her fashion prediction for the near future: a top made of canning labels encased in plastic with a black vinyl skirt. Terminal Velocity by Saand featured head gear and clothing of fragmented geometric shapes. Her architectural designs are made from shower curtains, melted plastic bowls, to marbleize oil painted nylon. One of her pieces was made entirely from television parts.

Wes Bond and Daniel Grimes of Fusion presented models wearing great oversized two-toned jumpsuits in red and blue with angular zippers.

Hank Ford, Executive Engineer for Del Ray Products recommends the removal and "burning of aged fabric exo-skins." She promotes the wearing of rubber, paper and vinyl, not to mention the "nasty nylon" skirt sported by Sony Skates, dominated by a molecular structure pattern. Also shown was an all white vinyl two-piece suit with zip-on jacket and pants.

Carl Wolf opened his segment with white paper jumpsuits (found at Supplies) which were ripped off to reveal his deep-cut, black vinyl tunic with yellow piping. His other model wore a shocking pink spandex mini with black hand-painted triangles.

10.1979, "Damage" #3
Fashion show
Photo Stephano Paolillo
(US fanzine)

Flammable Kitchen Fashions by Ray Gun (Nick'Urbaniak) represented his line with a clear vinyl skirt and backless top with plasticware encased in the plastic.

A black dress with multi-colored shapes sealed in plastic was one of the highlights of A. Marsh's second segment for Genetic Damage. The individual triangles are snapped on to the dress making them interchangeable. A straight, short-sleeved dress splashed with pink and white paint was accented with green surgical gloves, and tubing.

The bold use of geometric shapes, and simple lines makes an instant impact for the designs of Saxon. One of his designs featured an off-white tubular vest with extended circular arm openings, which were piped with quilted copper nylon with a retractable hood. Another model wore a scull-fitting black hat with a simple black strapless dress. Using polyurethane, nylon, cotton, lamé, among other, more rigid types of fabrics, Saxon uses sharp angled shapes (trapezoids, triangles, squares, etc.) to compliment the types of material used.

Making a big colorful splash in the show were the designs of Gary Miles, Barbara White and Susan Friedman for Japanese Weekend. They prefer to use 'fabrics of a natural fibre content which lends itself easily for imprinting purposes, and long, lasting wear.' Making FUN clothes is one of their biggest priorities. And that they are! Example: black cotton zip-on jacket with pink/black striped 'Bazooka Joe' collar, worn with black pants with side zippers. Versatility plays a big part in their clothing with zippers that can conceal or reveal a contrasting color...

Carol Alter of Supplies provided a fashion interrogation featuring clothing that can be found at her store. Models were presented with white drop-cloth sacks with the slogans "THIS YEAR'S COLOR," "THIS YEAR'S STYLE" painted on each. The sacks were shredded to reveal solid-color vinyl jumpsuits.

Stacatto Dysdain (a.k.a. Jeorgia A.) dominated the stage with her "fashion patrol" entourage carrying flashlights and wearing her structured vinyl clothes in bright colors. Accessorized with unusually high exaggerated collars, and multi-colored straps, the segment provided a striking visual statement.

Luther Blue, the "New York - comes - to - North Beach" store on Columbus Avenue was represented by Christeen (of the URGE), who was wearing a pair of royal blue vinyl two-piece suit. Cherry wore mint green vinyl chaps over a pair of spandex pants with matching top. Casey completed the space cowboy set with an eye-riveting reflecto vest and matching headband.

Genetic Damage, Japanese Weekend, Del Ray Prods, Stacatto Dysdain, and others can be found at Luther Blue (716 Columbus) and/or Supplies (3128 16th Street).

For more information about the Society, call (415) 397-3753.

FILE MEGAZINE TORONTO

FILE Megazine occupied pride of place in Toronto from 1972 to 1989. The renowned collective General Idea (which operated from 1969 to 1994) edited twenty-six issues of this sophisticated publication, which, although selfproduced, achieved broad distribution. The magazine's aim was to seek "an alternative to the alternative press," a subversive objective that required infiltrating mainstream media and culture. It was a quarterly written, modified, and published mainly by members of General Idea.

Content came in the form of contributions by correspondents via mail, which made *FILE* the first printed mail-art project. Each issue contained the contact info for key members of the network, including their pseudonyms (common practice at the time), as well as addresses.

With the withering of the mail-art movement, *FILE* expanded its scope, including articles on art and entertainment, with a particular focus on fashion and up-and-coming designers.

SHADES TORONTO

The fanzine *Shades*, based in Toronto and founded by George Dean Higton, was particularly well-structured and, like a real newspaper, boasted a proper staff of journalists, photographers and graphic designers. *Shades* was not just centered on music: it was interested in everything that happened in the city. Thanks to the journalist Lela Michael, illustrations of new fashion trends appeared in almost every issue.

12.1979, "Shades" #8
Leighton Barrett
Bouclé lace pants, Danger black vinyl gloves and Tube dress
Photo Steve Rasmussen
(Canadian fanzine)

In issue #8 (Dec. 1979), Lela told of a new look championed by designers like Leighton Barrett and his brand, Excel. It involved crocheted knitwear with striking color combos, such as blue-violet-fuchsia and red-pink-yellow; mohair sweaters in industrial tones like cement gray and metallic; and his "Bim-bam tunnel" clothes. *Shades* also included articles about Margherita Passion and her New Rose store, which featured sweaters imported from Britain, and handcrafted in the style of Johnny Rotten. There were also Algicyruss and extremely tightly-fitting pink fuchsia and cream dresses, as well as futuristic sweaters, spandex trousers, and jackets.

01-02.1979, "Shades" #8
Gerald Franklin's
Fall and Winter
Photo Andrée Gagné
(Canadian fanzine)

"AT 71 MCGAUL STREET IN THE VILLAGE BY THE GRANGE IS HOT COUTURE, WHERE GERALD FRANKLIN SHOWS HIS BEAUTIFUL CLOTHES AND INDEED WHERE MOST OF THEM ARE MADE.
IT IS NOT EASY TO GIVE AN IMPRESSION OF THE MAN BEHIND THE NAME AND PERHAPS IT IS NOT NECESSARY AS HE MAKES A VERY STRONG STATEMENT THROUGH HIS FASHIONS."

12.1979, "Shades" #8 (Canadian fanzine)

Shades continued into the eighties, and, thanks to its propensity to publish fashion articles, it provides a window into the rapid style changes that took place over that short timespan.

Between 1978 and 1980, issue after issue of *Shades* manifested metamorphoses in punk fashion, tangible transformations year after year. Such changes shook Toronto, just as they did the rest of the world.

In 1980, *Shades* featured a piece on the Gerald Franklin store: the ripped, threadbare T-shirts with incendiary symbols and slogans were giving way to extremely neat, well-cut outfits. The lines became clean, simple, minimal; black and white predominated, replacing shocking-pink and the hazardous combinations of caustic colors characteristic of the previous phase. And yet, there were still stylized ads for Amelia Earhart Originals (secondhand togs) and Rainbow Room, the beauty salon "that prepares you for the eighties."

CLOSED
RAINBOW ROOM
Consultants in Hair Design
1060 Yonge
967-644

Scene Recently at
RAINBOW ROOM
967-6442
1060 YONGE

MODERN CLOTHING
FOR MEN & WOMEN
ASK ABOUT OUR RENTAL SERVICE
PERIOD CLOTHING FROM VICTORIAN TO PUNK
AMELIA 1 · 99 Yorkville (cumberland Court)
AMELIA 2 · 535 Parliament (at Winchester)
920-5926
Amelia Earhart

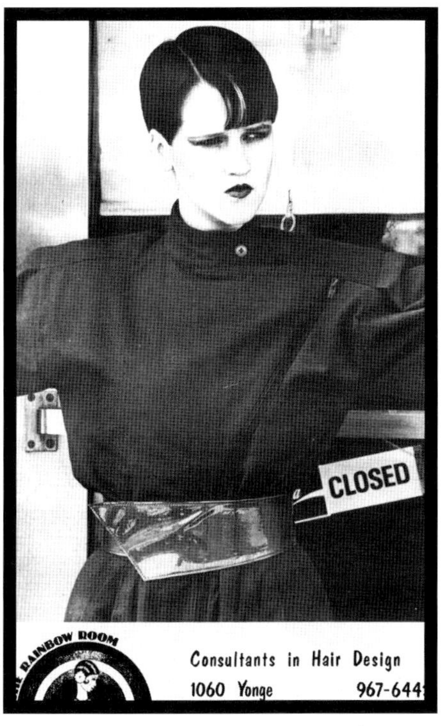

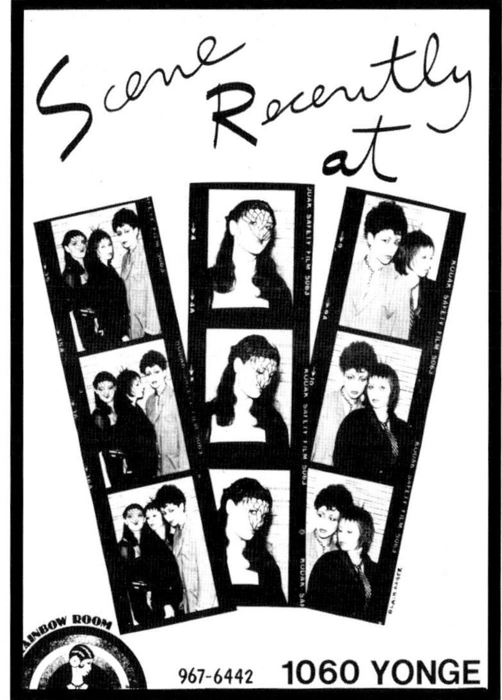

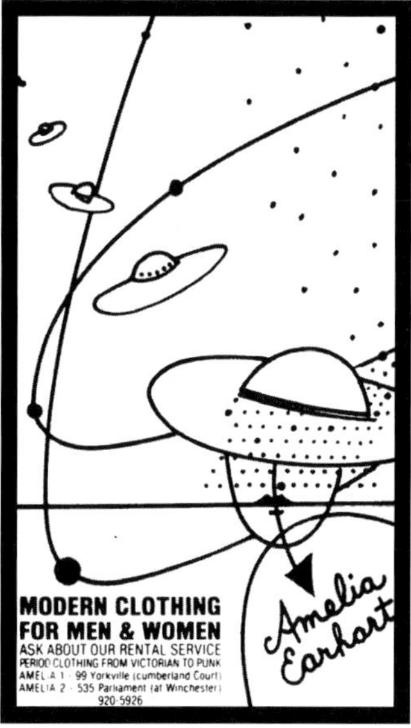

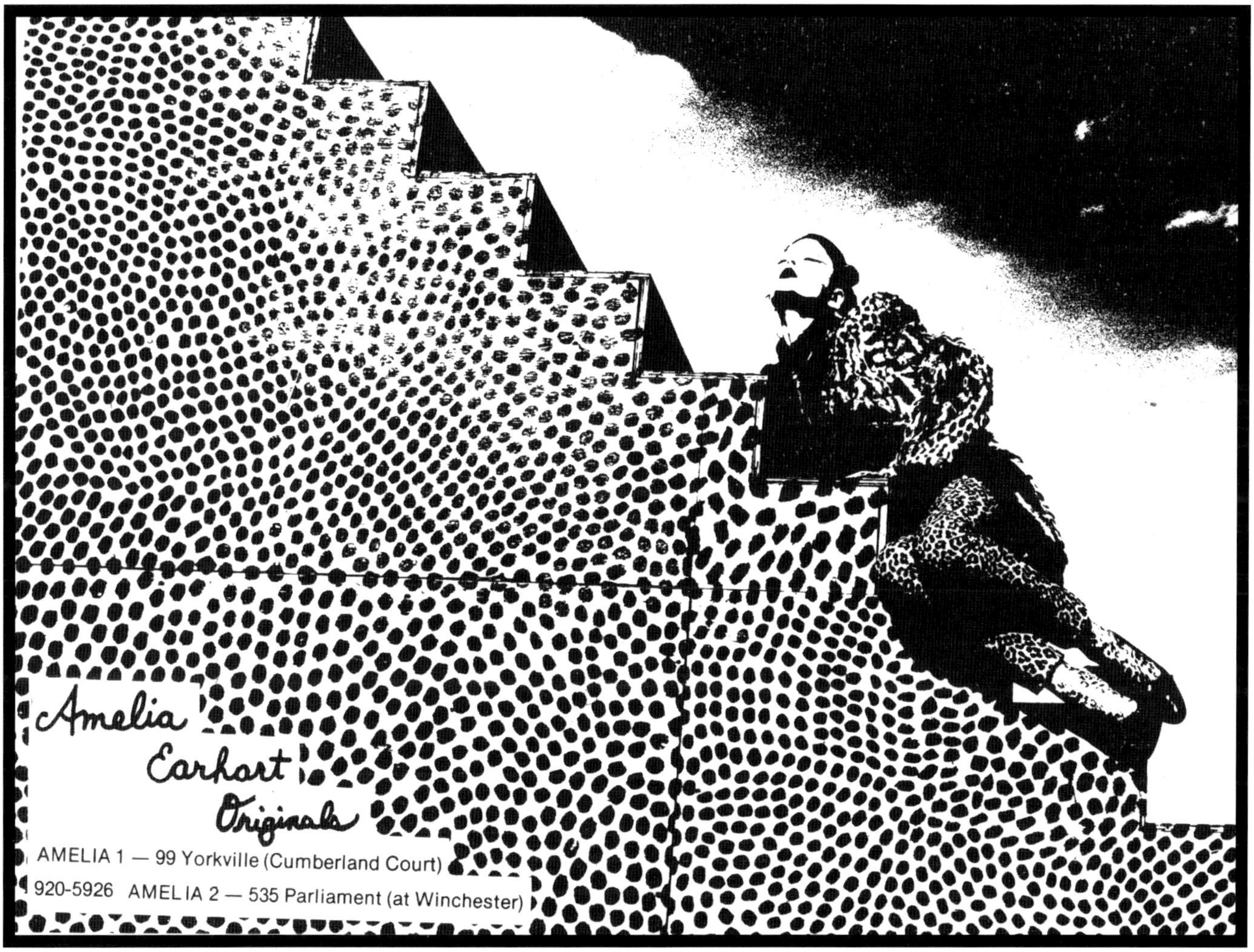

Amelia Earhart Originals
AMELIA 1 — 99 Yorkville (Cumberland Court)
920-5926 AMELIA 2 — 535 Parliament (at Winchester)

C'MON EVERYBODY. ORDER FAST! FOR XMAS
FOR WHOLESALE AND TRADE ENQUIRIES PLEASE WRITE TO US FOR OUR PROMPT ATTENTION
WE APOLOGISE TO CUSTOMERS AWAITING OUR CATALOGUE – DELAYS ARE DUE TO EVER INCREASING STOCK!!
VISIT OUR RETAIL SHOP AT 62 MIDLAND ROAD BEDFORD
PRICE FOR SUIT £39·95
ORIGINAL & COLOURFAST T's
MOD DESIGNS
CUSTOMER SERVICE DEPT.
GRINGO CASUALS CO. DEPT. SH 55, ST. PETER'S STREET, BEDFORD, BEDS. TEL: (0234) 58355
CODE | ALT | SIZE | COLOUR | T SHIRT CODE | DESIGN CODE | ALT. DESIGN
NAME & ADDRESS.
ORDER NOW!!
PAYMENT ENCLOSED £
ALSO

A BUMPER COMMERCIAL BOOM

The press didn't just inform: the music weeklies included ads for mail-order purchases (the forerunner to online shopping). In 1979 British pop-zine *Smash Hits* advertised the latest wares of Gringo Casuals Co. of Bedford: punk and mod T-shirts, striped or leopard drainpipes, bondage gear, cool shades, natty belts and ties…

Meanwhile, a similar set up increasingly pervaded the three major UK music papers: *Sounds*, *Record Mirror* and *New Musical Express*.

From Gringo Casuals you could buy the complete Clash look: Adam Ant's swashbuckler jacket; Devo's yellow jumpsuit, and energy dome hats. Joly MacFie's Better Badges created a cornucopia of punk pins. Within a year of its founding in 1976, the company had festooned the kingdom's punk populace with button-badges (spurred on by the Mont de Marsan Festival in May '77). It soon cornered this lucrative market, exporting millions of badges worldwide.

As Better Badges became economically successful, MacFie was able to venture into the publication and distribution of key fanzines like *Jamming*, *No Cure*, and *Panache*. He would also found an influential Londonwide pirate radio station, as well as the timorously titled label *Fuck Off* Records.

Punk's original DIY ethic became largely neglected, overshadowed by this expropriating breed of mail-order businesses offering a panoply of ready-made 'authentic' punk merchandise. Ads for bondage or PVC trousers, leopard-skin jackets (and even underwear), jewelry, badges, studded leather wristbands, occupy page after page of the major UK music weeklies, potentially turning readers into cut-out shop dummies.

Anyone could play at 'dress the punk mannequin,' a lackluster anti-DIY for your own body (marketed to the masses ad hoc):

1. These are the products;
2. Choose;
3. Compose your personalized look;
4. Pay by check or postal order;
5. Your order will be posted directly to your door.

Commercially, mail-order punk was a booming success.

Soon, the eighties arrived, and the stimuli provided by these dynamic, contradictory initiatives transmuted into a new style of music and clothes: amenable to everyone, brazenly commercial, easy to wear. Gone were the edgy ugliness and hostility that had characterized punk culture a couple of years ago. These were revamped products targeted a segmented teen market: rude boys, soul boys, mods and modettes, rockabillies, goths, new romantic pirate dandies, etc.

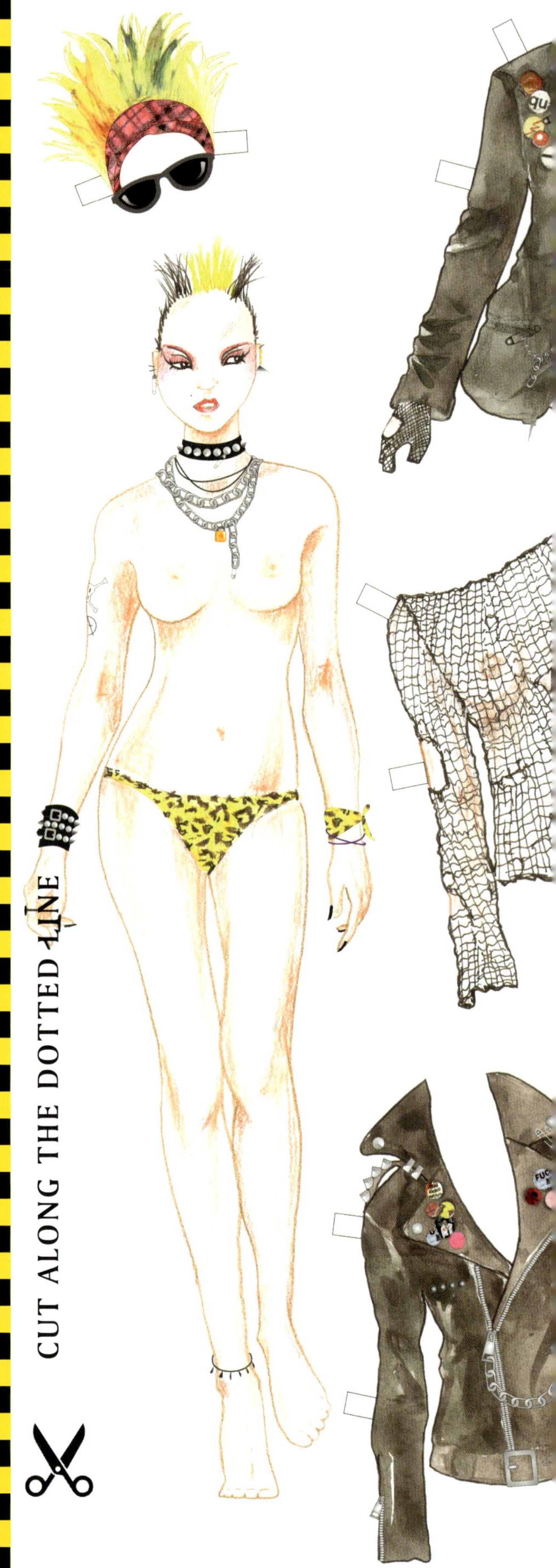

2018, Paper dolls
- UK street style
- Sex Pistols and Vivienne Westwood
- Devo "the American avant-garde"
- Two Tone Ska
- Pirates, buccaneers and tropical new romantics

Illustrations Paola Querin

CUT ALONG THE DOTTED LINE

FOR THE FUTURE
DUTY NOW
DEVO
SEX
original
DEVO
CUT ALONG THE DOTTED LINE

DEVO
DEVO
DEVO
D
DEVO
DEVO
D
CUT ALONG THE DOTTED LINE

CUT ALONG THE DOTTED LINE

CUT ALONG THE DOTTED LINE

FIORUCCI NIGHTMARE

By the early 1980s, the confounding commercialization of punk attire, in all its aesthetic derivatives — ska, goth, new romantic — was fully underway. But note how some shapes and colors characteristic of that original deviant look would start to recur in the shop windows, even of high-street chains. Fiorucci was the first international brand to host stylistic elements of pure punk pedigree in its streetwear collection.

Fiorucci is an exceptional fashion label, opening its first store in Milan, branching out overseas to London in 1975, New York in 1976 (where the store was designed by architects Ettore Sottsass, Andrea Branzi and Franco Marabelli), and Los Angeles by 1979. Elio Fiorucci evaluated and absorbed every novelty he encountered and was masterful at transforming them into coveted style items.

He mixed the glitter of Studio 54's disco scene with postmodern geometric shapes, and pop art with New York graffiti artists. From punk he not only imbibed the fluorescence and clashing colors but also the synthetic plastics, rubbers, and vinyls, as well as bondage elements, fanzine-style graphics, and fabric patterns of all strains, combining them to create new compositions.

GREGORY POE BECAME NOTED AS A FASHION VIRTUOSO FOR HIS INTRIGUING RANGE OF PLASTIC CLOTHING AND ACCESSORIES INCORPORATING VARIOUS UNUSUAL ADD-ONS: COLORFUL TOY FISH FLOATING IN WATERPROOF POCKETS AND HANDBAGS WITH CANDY WRAPPERS SEWN INTO THE SEAMS. THESE KITSCH ITEMS, WHICH WERE SNAPPED UP EAGERLY, WERE ON DISPLAY AT THE FIORUCCI BOUTIQUE ON MELROSE AVENUE, L.A.

1980, Fiorucci
New York store window
Photo Meredith Jacobson Marciano

>
1978, "Stuff "#3
Fiorucci publicity
Photo Carla Weber
(US fanzine)

Gregory Poe
FIORUCCI
EVERLY HILLS

1978, Fiorucci
New York store window
Photo Meredith Jacobson Marciano

The boutique's ironic window displays were a rich mélange of suggestiveness, including plush pink handcuffs, shockingly lurid garments, a recasting of the biker's peak cap in vinyl rather than black leather, stretch jeans, and extremely tight synthetic trousers, just to name a few as the list was endless.

In the November 1977 issue of *Playmen* (Italy's answer to *Playboy*), photographer Roberto Rocchi depicted punk fashion in an article entitled "Heil Punk!". The models paraded bare-chested; posed with their buttocks on display, dressed in chains, safety pins, shiny swastikas, and other overtly Nazi-inspired regalia: what little they wore was strictly Fiorucci.

The captions read: "Vietnam green quilted and padded nylon jacket, red T-shirt and white jeans. Shiny black faux leather raincoat, boxer shorts; another model wears a synthetic leopard tank top and jeans with a snake motif applied to the leg and also faux leather for the pants which are paired with a yellow string T-shirt, all by Fiorucci."

This unsigned feature was appalling, a presumptuous effort to inscribe the new fashion within the realm of a nightmarish credo: "And so the young, in the wake of the rock revival (exacerbated by the recent death of the 'King' Elvis Presley), wallow in their punk 'disguises': a sort of contamination between Red Indian war paint, Nazi nostalgia, second-rate sadomasochism (trashy remake of *The Night Porter*) and proliferation of chains, medals, faked wounds, fancy dress, violent colors, symbols (more or less on open display), swastikas, and, of course, sex, bare breasts, stiff nipples."

So, Fiorucci implied, young punks were all depraved nostalgic Nazis in various states of undress! A few months later, an article by Loredana Sottile, "La moda punk in Italia," appeared in *Nuovo Sound* with in-depth arguments on punk and fashion that served as a timely riposte to *Playmen's* "Heil Punk!"

"Speaking of the diverse aspects of Punk Rock, we must not forget another, perhaps less key, yet still characteristic, element of punk music and fashion, which, especially here in Italy, is one of the major facets of the whole panic. This is due to the error we have already tackled: to mistake punk rock for a political movement. It has been adopted above all by right-wing circles, becoming an identification of sorts for this fraction of Italian youth. [...] As you might have gathered, more than anything else, this movement became a bone of contention, after Fiorucci, the renowned high-end Italian fashion designer, who has always been inspired by youth culture, found it amusing to create a fashion line that imitated punk motifs. Unfortunately, Fiorucci has been at the center

11.1977, "Playmen"
Heil Punk!
Photo Roberto Rocchi
(Italian magazine)

of a misunderstanding from the start; his fashion line has been interpreted as a political declaration, causing many problems for him as well as specialist retailers. We had the opportunity to speak to someone from Fiorucci's press office in Milan. At first he was reluctant to talk about Punk, precisely because it has become such a delicate topic, but in the end he agreed to respond: 'Fiorucci has no political intent, Punk is a mass phenomenon, with social intent, and it is this aspect of Punk that Fiorucci was inspired by, also because he sold Punk long before it assumed any political taint, as it has subsequently here in Italy.'

At this point, we will allow readers to draw their own conclusions: so, over to you — *New Sound* is at your disposal."

By the end of the seventies, three thousand outlets lauded the genius of the Italian designer, who was able to blend complementary styles and cultures, a flair that on occasion resulted in misunderstanding and was sometimes judged as deplorable, even by the most radical of punks.

1980 saw the release of an EP by Washington, D.C. punk band The Teen Idles: it contains the track "Fiorucci Nightmare."

1978, Fiorucci
Window display, Beverly Hills, Los Angeles
Photo Meredith Jacobson Marciano

1978, Fiorucci
Window display, New York
Photo Meredith Jacobson Marciano

FIORUCCI NIGHTMARE, ASSHOLE'S DREAM
SPEND ALL YOUR MONEY ON THE FASHION MACHINE
SPOTS AND STRIPES AND SPANDEX PANTS
PAY A HUNDRED DOLLARS TO LEARN HOW TO DANCE

SPEND FIFTY DOLLARS ON A SWEATER
THINK IT'S GONNA MAKE YOU LOOK BETTER
SEE HOW TIGHT YOUR PANTS WILL FIT
WHAT YOU GONNA DO WHEN THEY START TO SPLIT

LEARN YOUR FASHION FROM A MAGAZINE
DO YOU REALLY THINK YOU'RE IN OUR DREAMS
DOWN IN GEORGETOWN IN A FASHION RACE
FOR THE GUYS TO SEE HOW HIGH YOU RATE

"Fiorucci Nightmare"
The Teen Idles

1978, Fiorucci, store interior
Beverly Hills, Los Angeles
Photo Meredith Jacobson Marciano

PERESTROIKA WAVE

That which had been born in the UK and USA grew rapidly and spread throughout the English-speaking world. For other countries, such as Italy, Spain and Portugal, the punk trend was adopted by a mere scattering of tiny cliques until the early eighties. Here, for practical reasons, it was still a DIY look, whilst throughout the Anglo-sphere it had turned into a highly commercialized phenomenon.

However, what occurred in Eastern Europe's communist states was different and particularly intriguing. In the Soviet Union, before perestroika, the state endeavored to control all aspects of life; music and any associated, alternative lifestyle were actively discouraged. Everything was under harsh supervision. It wasn't until 1985 that suppressed music and styles of dress began to emerge from out of the shadows.

1987, Vilnius, Lituania
Punk band Nautilus Pompilus.
Sverdlovsk Rock Club dressing room
Photo Igor Moukhin

Tupie (meaning "stupid")
One of the funniest Muscovite punk bands.
Photo taken in 1988 at a gig in Zelenograd
(backstage in the dressing room)
Natasha (left) Dunya Smirnova (right)
Both in dance troupe pose.
Photo Igor Moukhin

We can peek into this world through the images of photographer Igor Moukhin, who recorded young Moscow and Leningrad punks going about their daily lives. The photos date back to 1986, a sort of "year zero"; the kids look similar to those who appeared at the London Roxy Club ten years before: individualism, DIY attire, recycling, and ready-mades were popular — "the revenge of anti-fashion!"

Soviet youth substituted the unattainable DMs of Western punks for combat boots from Voentorg, a Soviet-wide chainstore specializing in military gear. Ditto for jackets: black naval jackets were very popular buys from Voentorg, along with medals and other Soviet military regalia. Of course, how they were then displayed was another story altogether.

1987, Moscow
In those years Arbat was the first and only pedestrian street in the USSR, a meeting place for many youth groups.
Photo Igor Moukhin

"PODOLSK IS A CITY NEAR MOSCOW. IN 1987 I WORKED ON A LOCAL MUSIC FANZINE CALLED 'ZOMBIE', SAMIZDATSTYLE, SELF-PRODUCED (HANDMADE), WITH LOTS OF IMAGES, REPORTAGE, PHOTOGRAPHIC PORTRAITS OF ROCK STARS, INTERVIEWS.

ONLY ONE COPY OF THE FANZINE CAME OUT, BUT IN THE ENVIRONMENT OF ROCK PARTIES IT WAS ENOUGH. THE TEXTS WERE REPRINTED ON TYPEWRITERS WITH CARBON-COPY PAPER, SO THE WHOLE USSR READ THE MAGAZINE!!!

THERE IS A PRESENTATION OF A NEW MAGNETI ALBUM AND IN THE ROOM ARE TEN TO TWELVE GUESTS WHO CAME FROM THE UNDERGROUND ROCK SCENE; THE VENUE IS A SMALL CLUB OF FORTY TO FIFTY SEATS. I CAN TAKE A SERIOUS RALPH GIBSON STYLE PHOTO, A SEMINAL EXERCISE WITH LIGHT."

Igor Moukhin

>
1987, Podolsk
Photo Igor Moukhin

1986, Leningrad
Cultural Center dress room,
where the annual rock festival takes place.
The punk showman Oleg Garkusha talks to
his girlfriend.
Photo Igor Moukhin

From Los Angeles to Moscow, the same rule applied: everything could be re-used.

We will see that in detail over the following pages, through testimonies from that time and photos taken between 1976 and 1986 by various photographers in different cities around the world: evidence that helps us retrace the first ten years of this socio-cultural phenomenon, from its birth and commercial explosion through its demise.

1979, Downtown Fashion
New York
Photo Edo Bertoglio

1976-1980, San Francisco
Photo Jimmy Jocoy

10-11 1977, New York
Design Liz Kurtzhan
(US fanzine)

$ 4,000.00
DESIGNER
TOP
ELIZABETH
ARDEN
SAFETY-PIN
SCAR
COVER-UP
JACKIE PUTRID
MONOPOLY IN THE
PASTE-ON
X-TRA
LONG
NAILS
RT.
LT.
RT.
LT.
ATTATCH
TO LEG
A SHOE?
FOLD
•LIZ KURTZMAN

HAIR STY LE

CUT, DYE & MESS-UP

CCCP FEDELI ALLA LINEA
ORAZIO
ALI MACGRAW
LOVE STORY
PEGGY LIPTON
MOD SQUAD
WET
NEW YORK ROCKER
HAIR POWER
DEBRA EVANS
CARLOS MANFREDI
PAUL MCGREGOR
JANE FONDA
BREE DANIELS
KLUTE
JOAN JETT
DAVID CASSIDY
VIDAL SASSOON
FARRAH FAWCETT
CHARLIE MILLER
MAUREEN
DAVID DARLING
RIZIA
CORNICHE
CRAZY COLOR
MR. ROGER OF BIRMINGHAM
PETER K'S SALONS LTD.
PAOLO OF FLORENCE
FRANCO-LEICESTER
DOMENICK AND TONY
MARK YOUNG
BRUNO OF ITALY
MARK YOUNG
GENERATION X
PETER GRAVELLE
SIOUXIE SIOUX
DEBBIE HARRY
BLONDIE
KOOL-AID
KIA-ORA
JIMMY JOCOY

1977 CRAZY COLOR LONDON

RENBOW (UK, LONDON)
ROGER OF MISS RAYMOND
ECLIPSE
STEVE SANDON
DARRYLL
JORDAN
MASAYOSHI SUKITA
FAB HAIRCUTS
NART
KENNY BERK
DAUL MILKIE
BARBARA FARMAN
BETSY JOHNSON

1979 PLASMATICS BOSTON

THE PARADISE
WENDY O. WILLIAMS
JEAN BEAUVOIR
RICHARD PARSONS

NEO-HAIRCUTS LOS ANGELES

ATILA SIKORA
SLASH
PIPER CLUB
DINO IGNANI

1985 JEAN PHILIP PAGÈS PARIGI

FRIGIDAIRE
ANTONIO CARMELO EROTICO
PIPER CLUB
DINO IGNANI

OLY'S

HAIRCUTTING

MAKE-UP

MANICURES

PERMANENTS

NATURAL COLORING

210 E. 21 ST., N.Y.

212-673-2800

Consultants in Hair Design

967-6442

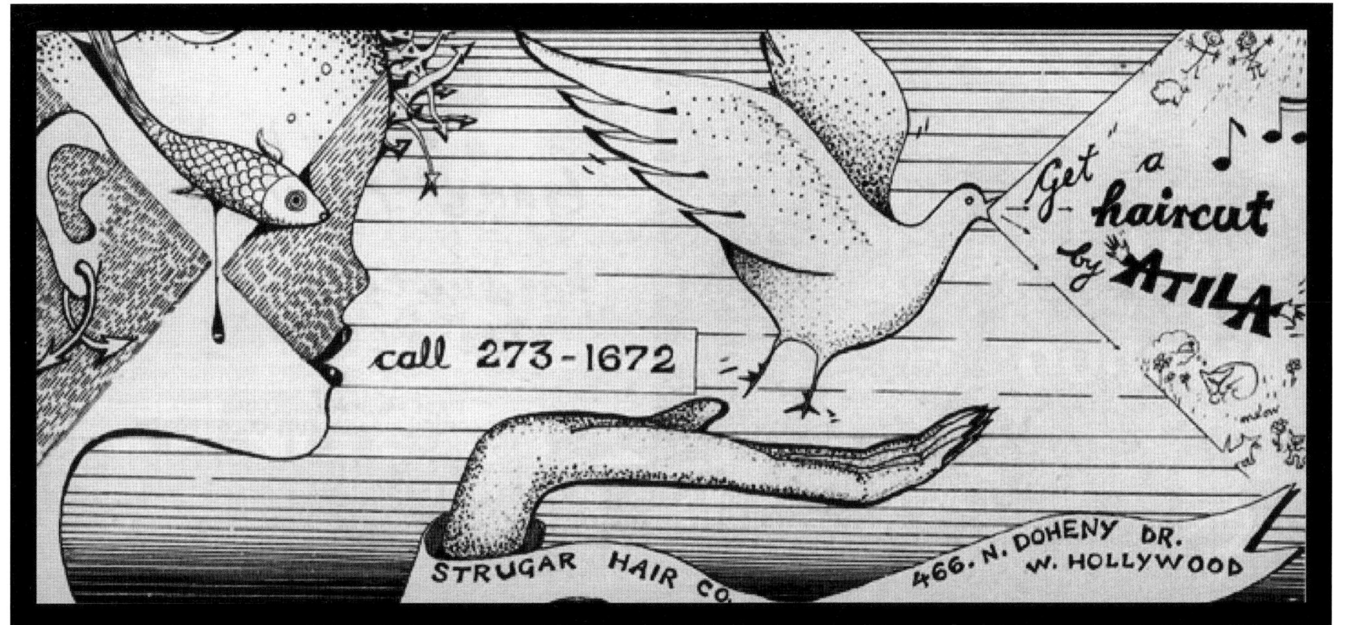
Get a haircut by ATILA
call 273-1672
STRUGAR HAIR CO.
466. N. DOHENY DR.
W. HOLLYWOOD

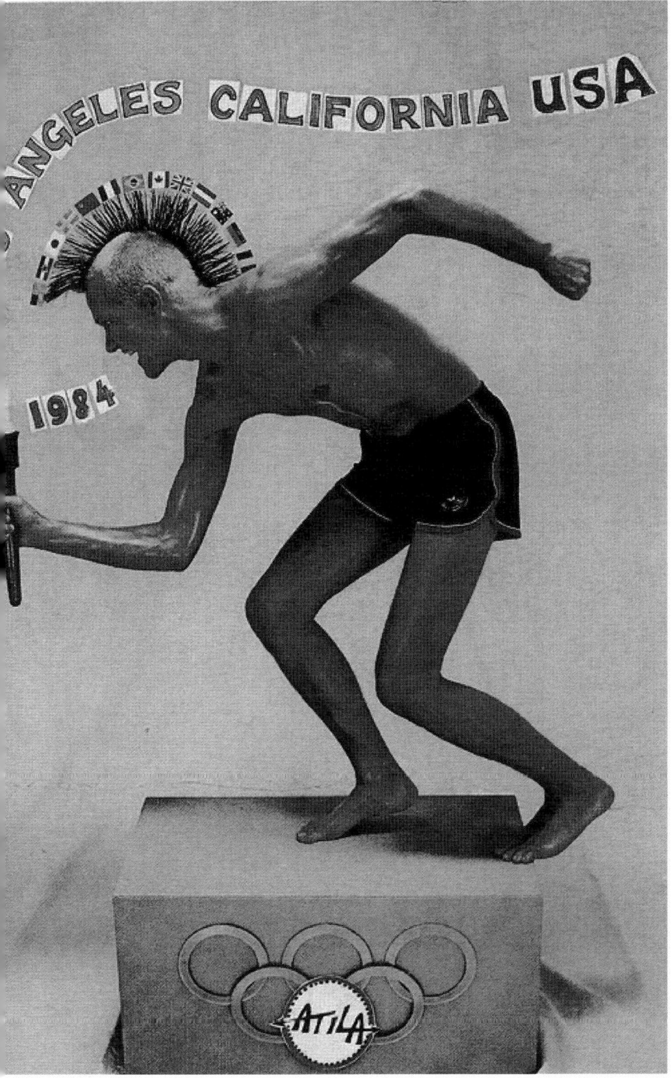
ANGELES CALIFORNIA USA
1984
ATILA

NARCISSUS
X Y
Z
APPOINTMENTS: 775-4972
A B
C
LOOK GOOD
KRAZYKOLOR TINTS DYES XTREMITY

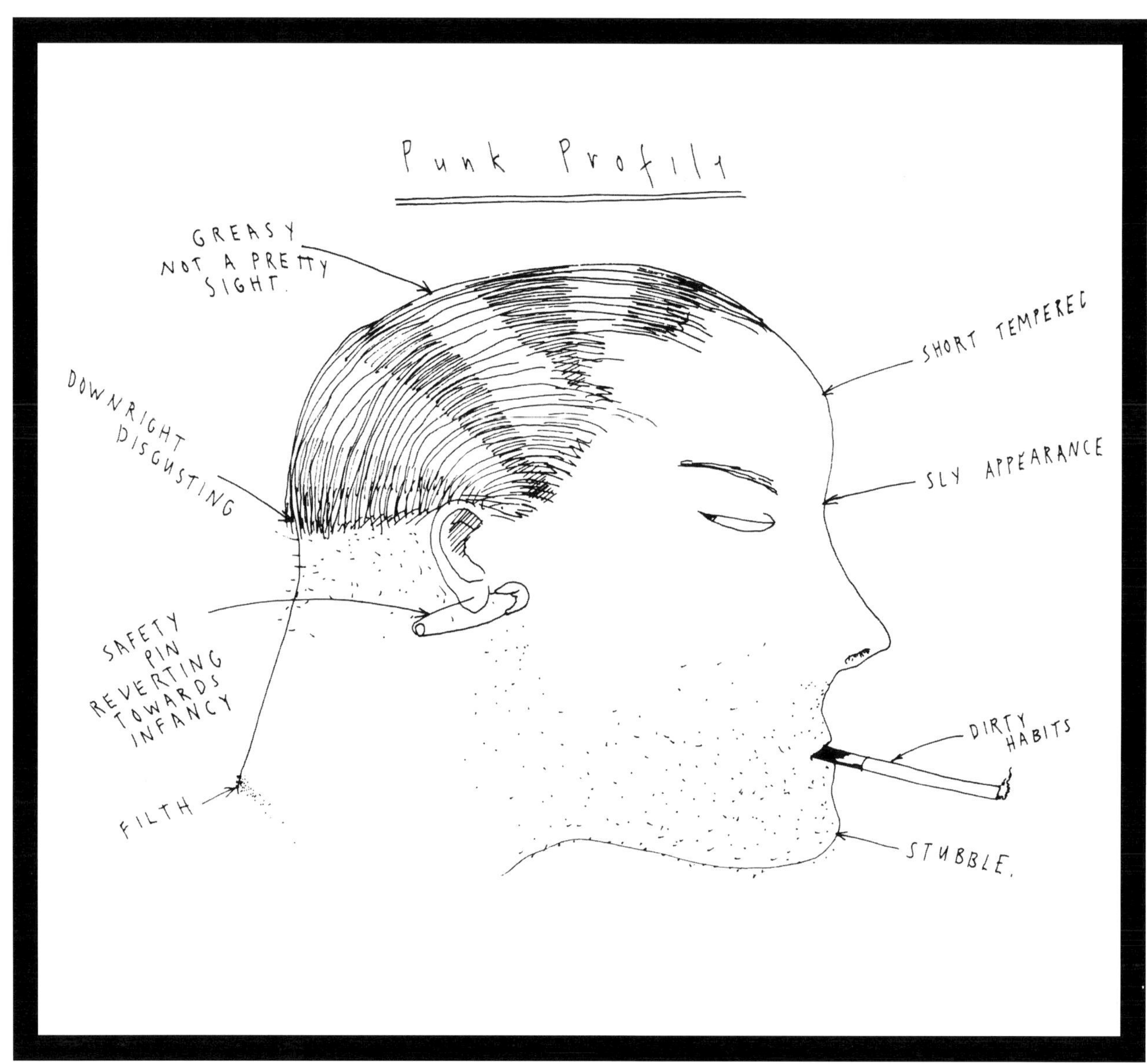

08.1978, Illustration from "WET"
(US magazine)

CUT, DYE & MESS-UP

“BETTER A MEDICATION OR AN INFERNAL STORY? BETTER IDLE DAYS OR GREEN HAIR?”

Cccp Fedeli alla linea (TRANSLATION)

Young adult hair styles show originality and pride of appearance

From the dawn of civilization, scissors have sculpted heads around the world. Way before a head of green hair had been imagined, other oddities were in style. By the beginning of the 2nd century BC, the Romans were using shears to cut hair, though the instrument had not yet been perfected to render a uniform cut. Over a century later, Horace quipped, making fun of himself: “*Si curatus inaequali tonsore capillos occurri, rides,*” meaning, “With my hair cut in an uneven manner, you snicker.”

In ancient China, cutting hair was a disgrace, while Roman soldiers wore beards and short hair in order to prevent their enemies from having something to grasp onto; in France, long hair was a rare privilege allotted to kings and nobles.

By the 1960s and ‘70s, by contract, there were so many styles in vogue that it is tricky to outline them. However, a common style amongst younger kids was very straight, long hair separated by a central part, in the style of Ali MacGraw in *Love Story* (1970) or Peggy Lipton in the hit US television series *The Mod Squad* (1968-1973).

06-07.1977, “New York Rocker”
Publicity
(US magazine)

1976, HairPower Advert
Debra Evans
Photo Carlos Manfredi

By the sixties, a wide-ranging assortment of hair-smoothing paraphernalia was on the market, convenient for all budgets, multiple weird and wonderful accessories to shape the swinging styles.

Popular among British girls were "Wings," a wavy, combed-over fringe with hair flipping out winglike around the ears. In the early seventies, "The Ape" was all the rage: shorter hair on top was combined with longer hair in the back. Straight or curly hair was thoroughly layered to achieve a willfully ragged look.

Concurrently, coming in at number two: "The Shag," devised by hairstylist Paul McGregor for Jane Fonda's role in *Klute* (1971), was a simple, unisex cut in which the hair was layered and feathered to various lengths, creating a full crown with thinner fringes. Longer versions were worn by the likes of David Cassidy and Joan Jett.

By the mid-seventies, especially in the UK, Vidal Sassoon's "Bob Cut" bounced into a disco beat. The bowl-cut "Pageboy" (or "Purdey") followed onto the dance floor, chased by "Flicks and Wings" on rollerskates (the Farrah Fawcett look), and then, by the end of the seventies, a more sophisticated asymmetrical trend, prevalent in high fashion: locks were longer on one side, often gathered in a ponytail, either high above the ear or lower down at the shoulder.

Antithetical to straight hair, "The Afro" also became very fashionable. Black people embraced their natural curls or braided their hair tightly into cornrows. These hairstyles represented an awakening of community pride. White people, too, could be seen adopting these styles as a sign of solidarity and protest.

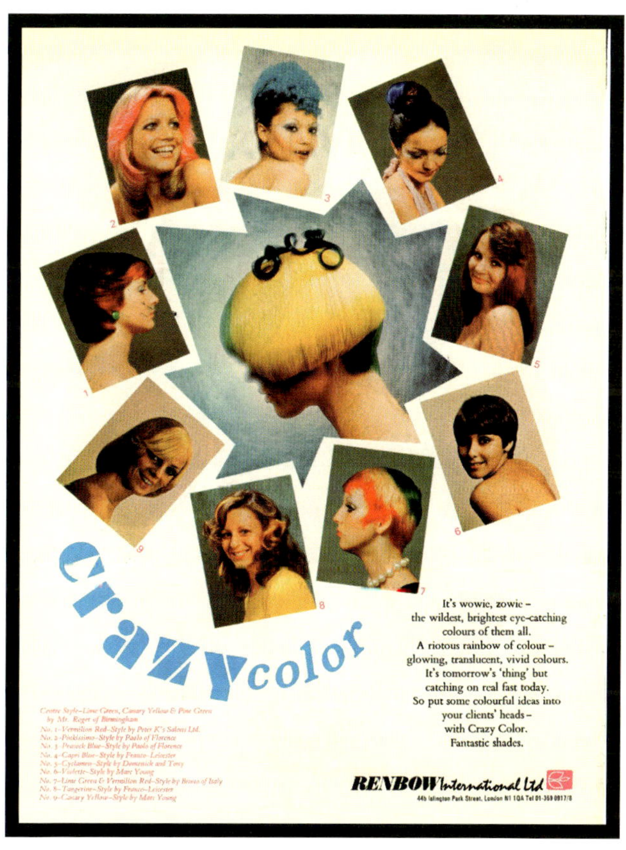

Late-1970s, Crazy Color catalog
Hairstyle Charlie Miller
Color Maureen
Photo David Darling
Makeup Rizia
Clothes Corniche

Late-1970s, Crazy Color catalog (clockwise text)
Centre Style – Lime Green, Canary Yellow & Pine Green by Mr. Roger of Birmingham
No. 1 – Vermilion Red – Style by Peter K's Salons Ltd.
No. 2 – Pinkissimo – Style by Paolo of Florence
No. 3 – Peacock Blue – Style by Paolo of Florence
No. 4 – Capri Blue – Style by Franco-Leicester
No. 5 – Cyclamen – Style by Domenick and Tony
No. 6 – Violette – Style by Marc Young
No. 7 – Lime Green & Vermilion Red – Style by Bruno of Italy
No. 8 – Tangerine – Style by Franco-Leicester
No. 9 – Canary Yellow – Style by Marc Young

1977, Generation X
Photo Peter Gravelle

And then punk happened: hair was there to shock, to be a mangy mess, like fur on a stray cat after a night of rough sex.

Despite not being adopted by the masses, the punk coiffure played a significant role in the history of hairdressing of the period. Punk hairstyles were short, angular, and disheveled; the opposite of long, affably rounded "hippie hair."

The Mohican, which became the icon of the 1980s punk movement, can still be seen at concerts, pogoing alongside shaved heads and fifties quiffs. Mohawks are crests that defy gravity, held fast not only by means of lacquers and gels, but also with household ingredients like egg, sugarwater, soap.

Hair could be dyed vivid colors or Siouxsie Sioux's raven black or Debbie Harry peroxide blond. Crazy Color, which was opportunely launched in 1977, was the go-to solution in the UK, but other products were available; food coloring and even soft drinks, such as Kool-Aid and Kia-Ora, were utilized.

With two packets of powdered Kool-Aid (without sugar) and two cups of water in a pan, it was feasible to brew interesting, low-cost colors, based on the flavors advertised: red (cherry), pink (raspberry), blue (blueberry) and violet (grape). For a more faded look, just dilute the concoction to taste.

Patterns flourished, too, like leopard spots and tiger stripes and everything in between. As was the prevailing mood, unisex styles dominated.

1976-1980, San Francisco
Photo Jimmy Jocoy

1977
CRAZY COLOR LONDON

Crazy Color, a vegetable-based coloring cream manufactured by Rembow (London, UK), launched in 1977, mid-punk explosion. Since then, it has become a respected brand — something of a cult product globally. "It's wowie, zowie the wildest, brightest eye-catching colours of them all. A riotous rainbow of colour ~ glowing, translucent, vivid colours. It's tomorrow's 'thing' but catching on real fast today. So put some colourful ideas into your clients' head with Crazy Color. Fantastic shades."

Hairstyle
Roger of Miss Raymond, Birmingham (UK)
for Renbow

Late 1970s, Crazy Color catalog
Hairstyle Eclipse
Makeup Darryll
Photo Steve Sandon

"Nart" #1
Advert for Fab Haircuts
(US fanzine)

>
1977, Jordan
Photo Masayoshi Sukita

1977, London
Photo Masayoshi Sukita

Hairstyle Kenny Berk
Photo Daul Milkie
Makeup Barbara Farman
Clothes Betsy Johnson

1979
PLASMATICS
BOSTON

05.1979, Plasmatics
The Paradise - Boston
Wendy O. Williams on tour with lead guitarist Richie Stotts, who is sporting a mohawk, not yet dyed.
Stotts was certainly amongst the first pioneers of this hairstyle, which became a punk standard over the course of the 1980s.
Photo Richard Parsons

>
05.1979, Plasmatics
Wes Beech at The Paradise - Boston
Photo Richard Parsons

PLASMATICS

NEO-HAIRCUTS LOS ANGELES

FOR A MOHAWK OR A SHAVED HEAD WITH PURPLE STRIPES, THERE WAS ATILA SIKORA, WHO WORKED AT 5255 MELROSE AVE., HOLLYWOOD IN THE EARLY EIGHTIES.
AN ECCENTRIC AND EXTRAVAGANT ODDBALL, HE WAS, WITH HIS RAZOR, THE PIED PIPER OF PUNK CUTS IN THE CITY.

11.1979, "Slash"
(US fanzine)

ZZZ
ON
464-
8920
GENESIS
THES
NEO-HAIR CUTS
HOLLYWOOD
$15
257 MELROSE 5255
ATILA '80

Rome
Piper Club, mid-eighties
Photo Dino Ignani

1985
JEAN PHILIP PAGÈS, PARIS

"I'M NOT A PUNK, NOR AN ANTI-PUNK. I'M A HAIRDRESSER WHO LOVES THE MATERIAL OF HIS WORK, WHO REFUSES TO TREAT IT IN AN EXCLUSIVELY TRADITIONAL WAY. I AM A CREATIVE WHO SAYS 'YES' TO HIS DESIRE TO EXPERIMENT."

Jean Philip

05.1985, "Frigidaire"
Hairstyle Jean Philip Pagès
Photo Antonio Carmelo Erotico
(Italian magazine)

Hairdressing performance
Piper Club, Rome
Mid-eighties
Photo Dino Ignani

MA
KE
UP

TRACE, WHITEN, BLACKEN

CLEOPATRA
THEDA BARA
DAVE VANIAN
DAMNED
ROXY CLUB
HARRY T. MURLOWSKY
SNIFFIN' GLUE #7
JIMMY JOCOY
RAT CLUB
MISS LYN
JEAN ARP
KANDINSKIJ
KLEE
ALKONET (ALKANNA TINCTORIA)
THUNA
LOLA MICHAEL
MARGHERITA
PASSION
CHERYL
NEELTJE
SHADES
CARRON
POSEUR
MEREDITH JACOBSON MARCIANO
JORDAN
LINDA ASHBY
ST JAMES HOTEL
BUCKINGHAM PALACE
SIMON BARKER AKA SIX
MASAYOSHI SUKITA
SIOUXSIE

1983 LEIGH BOWERY LONDON

BLITZ CLUB
CAMDEN PALACE
HEAVEN
BILLY'S
THE BATCAVE
CLUB TABOO
TONY GORDON
BOTTICELLI
BOTERO
FEDERICO FELLINI
GUY BARNES (AKATROJAN)
DAVID WALLS
DAVID GWINNUTT
ROYAL FESTIVAL HALL

THE EIGHTIES ROBYN BEECHE LONDON

VIVIENNE WESTWOOD
LEIGH BOWERY
STEVE STRANGE
DIVINE
RICHARD SHARAH
MICHAEL VOLBRECHT
VISAGE
VIDAL SASSOON
ELIZABETHAN RUFFS
PHYLLIS COHEN
RICHARD SHARPLES
TINA
ROXY CLUB
PETER GRAVELLE
ZANDRA RHODES

01.1977, Dave Vanian (The Damned)
Roxy Club, London
Photo Harry T. Murlowsky
For fanzine "Sniffin' Glue" #7

TRACE, WHITEN, BLACKEN

IN GENERAL THE SKIN SHOULD LOOK PALLID, RATHER THAN SUN-KISSED. THE PUNK SCENE IS PREDOMINANTLY AN URBAN ONE, REQUIRING SALLOW FACES; PUNKS ARE NOT SURFERS ENDOWED WITH SAND-DUNE SUNTANS.

The instinct to rebel, to stand out in a conformist society, and the buzz of being provocative were typical of the punk movement. This energy was also expressed through an approach to makeup, one that burned all bridges to the cosmetic rules of the past, then rebuilt them in order to highlight their oppressing force and cry for a freedom in which the only aesthetic was subversion. The face can function as just another urban wall on which to ink symbols and daub slogans.

Eyes were encircled with heavy eyeliner, which was extended to the sides of the face — a cinematographic reference to Cleopatra from the sixties or, conceivably, the vamp look of Theda Bara from the twenties. Vampire makeup took off too: a deathly white face contrasted by blackened rounds for the eyes worked just as eerily for either sex.

Two tones of blush were widely used to render a skull effect: a brighter tone on the cheekbone and darker one below traced and brought out the shape of the cheekbone, enhancing the overall punk pallor. Brown and rust-colored eyeshadow seemed to dominate, yet the whole of the eyelids were covered with at least two or three hues. Lipstick shades ranged from blood-red to jet-black.

1976-1980, San Francisco
Photo Jimmy Jocoy

04.1977, Dave Vanian (The Damned)
Rat Club, Boston
Photo Miss Lyn Cardinal

For brunettes, a combination of red, black, or gunmetal grey was better. Red was applied underneath the eyebrows with black shading around the eyes and outer area to recreate a bruised look. Metallic silvers, but not pearly whites, were used for sheen. For blondes, pure and intense colors helped the face stand out. Reddish-purple and rust with green were sound combinations.

Sometimes makeup was deliberately affected and, like theatrical face paint, was used to draw out a persona rather than to augment one's own countenance. Furthermore, faces could be embellished with insignia, strokes of paint or designs along the lines of Jean Arp, Kandinskij, and Klee.

Early on, Toronto punks availed themselves of dyer's alkanet roots *Alkanna tinctoria*, sought after for achieving particularly florid shades of red.

"[...] EXPLORE THUNA, THE HERBALIST AT 298 DANFORTH AVENUE. IF NOTHING ELSE TRY THEIR ALKONET CHIPS. SOAK SOME OF THESE IN ALCOHOL OVERNIGHT AND USE THE RESULTANT TINCTURE FOR BRIGHT RED CHEEKS OR FOR A BRILLIANT EYE MAKEUP EFFECT—GLAZE THE VERMILION EYE MAKEUP WITH A SLICK OF VASELINE [...]"

Suit Yourself by Lola Michael with Margarita Passion, Cheryl and Neeltje 10-11.79 "Shades" #7

1979, Carron inside the store Poseur
Los Angeles
Photo Meredith Jacobson Marciano

> 1976-1980, Los Angeles
Photo Jimmy Jocoy

1977, London
Photo Masayoshi Sukita

Jordan In Black Patent Dress
Linda Ashby's Flat
St James Hotel
Next Door to Buckingham Palace
Photo Simon Barker (aka Six)

1977-1978, Siouxsie - Makeup red
Linda Ashby's room
St James's Hotel, London
Near Buckingham Palace
Photo Simon Barker aka Six

1983
LEIGH BOWERY
LONDON

Part performance art, part fashion designer, Leigh Bowery was born in Australia in 1961, landed in London in the early eighties, and immediately became a reference point for music, style, and art. When punk fashion became a central force propelling youth culture, transforming and remodeling itself into divergent styles, nightclubs served as hubs for keeping abreast of what was going on. The Blitz club and then Camden Palace, Heaven, Billy's, The Batcave, and Taboo hosted the luminaries of a new wave of exoticism, a coterie of romantic airs and grace.

Bowery, who was invited by club entrepreneur Tony Gordon to front a night at Taboo, acted out desecrating rituals, which demonstrated his renewed commitment to punk. There, he regularly held court, wearing extreme makeup and eccentric selfembroidered clothes, continually subverting sexual norms. His look stitched together oriental art, plastic toys, Op-Art from the sixties, and fetish gear, along with allusions to bygone imagery from other realms: Botticelli, Botero, Fellini.

Bowery also created opulent costumes for his flatmates Guy Barnes (aka Trojan) and David Walls. The trio became known around town as the Three Kings.

1983, Leigh Bowery
Skirt dress
Farrell House, Ronald Street,
London E1,
Photo David Gwinnutt

1983, Leigh Bowery
Fur coat
Farrell House, Ronald Street,
London E1
Photo David Gwinnutt

1983, Leon Trojan
Foyer of the Royal
Festival Hall, London
Photo David Gwinnutt

>
1983, Leigh Bowery
Bedroom
London
Photo David Gwinnutt

OXBERRY

THE EIGHTIES ROBYN BEECHE LONDON

Robyn Beeche was a Sydney-based photographer who documented post-punk, new romantic fashion, and London's music scenes in the 1980s. She captured celebrities of the moment like Zandra Rhodes, Vivienne Westwood, Leigh Bowery, Steve Strange, and Divine. Her images fall somewhere between fashion and art: the use of heavy facial make-up and highly sophisticated lighting, tended to fragment, distort and transform bodies into something akin to a painted canvases or even sculpture.

<
1980, Divine
Makeup Richard Sharah
Kimono Michael Volbrecht
Photo Robyn Beeche

1980, Photo for record sleeve Visage - Fade to Grey
Steve Strange's makeup is by Richard Sharah
Photo Robyn Beeche

<

1986, Arrows from Vidal Sassoon Elizabethan Ruffs series
Makeup Phyllis Cohen
Arrow necklace Richard Sharples
Photo Robyn Beeche

1987, Tina
Makeup Phyllis Cohen
Photo Robyn Beeche

1977, Roxy Club, London
Photo Peter Gravelle

FOOT WE AR

SNEAKERS, DOCS, HIGH HEELS

DR. MARTENS
NAZIM MUSTAFAEV
RUSSIAN VIRTUAL SHOE MUSEUM
GRIGGS
BULLDOG BOOTS
GETTA GRIP
MAERTENS E FUNCK

BROTHEL CREEPERS

GEORGE COX
HAMILTON
NAZIM MUSTAFAEV
RUSSIAN VIRTUAL SHOE MUSEUM

WINKLEPICKERS

TEDDY BOYS

SHELLY'S

THE JAM

VIVIENNE WESTWOOD

PIRATE COLLECTION
NAZIM MUSTAFAEV
RUSSIAN VIRTUAL SHOE MUSEUM
BOY
SEDITIONARIES
PUNKPISTOL COLLECTION
RICHIE STOTTS
PLASMATICS
PARADISE ROCK CLUB
RICHARD PARSONS

PUNKS PUT THE BOOT IN AT

These patent leather stiletto boots with the cult ankle
safety pin buckle are made especially for anti-es
heroines! The rebel boot is available to Punk pu
following ground razing colour tones: Cream, Razor
Yellow, Orange, Bondage Black, Electric Blue. Size
same style and sizes but in kid leather. BOTH ANARC
PRICED **£19.99** + 25p P&P.

State size and colour (+ 2nd choice) when orde
Chqs/PO to:

Dept ME3 Bloggs, 187 Wardour St., London W1 Barclaycard & Ac
days delivery. Large selection of other models please wri

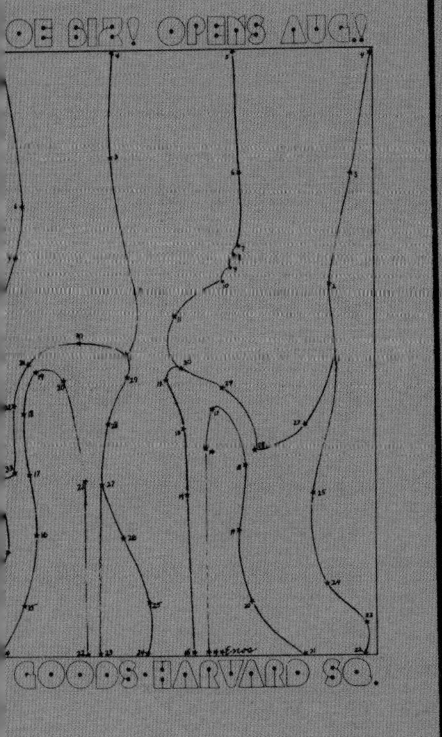

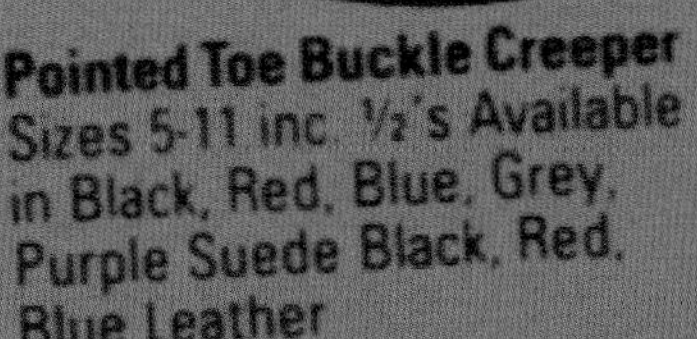

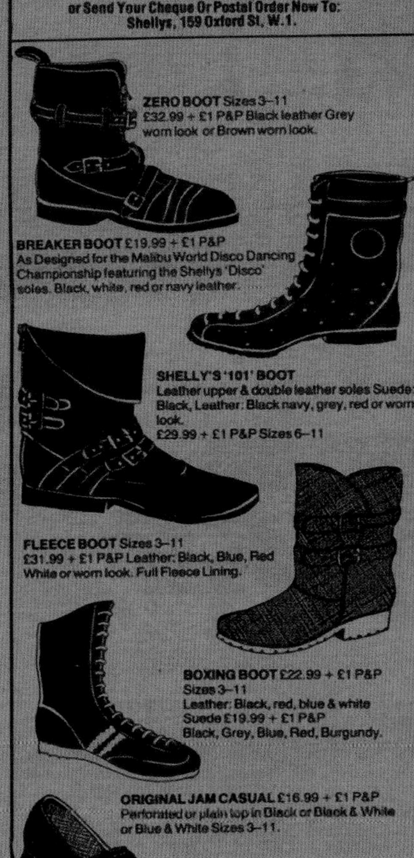

No. 1 IN FASHION SHELLYS SHOES
For Details Of Further Styles Of Boots And Shoes + Our Ladies Range
Send A SAE For Your Free Colour Catalogue To:
SHELLYS SHOES,
159 OXFORD ST, LONDON W.1.

Mid-seventies
High platform shoes in red patent-leather with three straps
Photo by kind permission of Nazim Mustafaev
Russian Virtual Shoe Museum

SNEAKERS, DOCS, HIGH HEELS

CANVAS SNEAKERS TENDED TO BE THE FOOTWEAR OF CHOICE BECAUSE THEY COULD BE SO EASILY CUSTOMIZED WITH FABRIC COLORANTS

A shoe is a richly versatile accessory: we can personalize our feet with any shape, color, and material. Ironic and open-minded punk, with its aesthetic of citing and reclaiming, drew enormously on a vast repertoire of forms and feels from the past. Well, so long as a style differentiated itself from the immediate past; hippy long hair, Afghan coats, flared trousers, and, indeed, certain footwear choices attributable to the flower power generation were strictly banished from the look — no to clogs, cowboy boots, leather sandals, and footwear over-decorated with charming trinkets!

In general, natural materials were avoided (with the exception of leather, especially fetish-inspired glossy black). Synthetic substances, plastics, and anything with artificially lurid colors were all ideally suited for the reality of this new modern world.

Women's shoes from the thirties, forties, and fifties, snapped up from second-hand shops or markets, were repainted ad hoc, as were platform shoes, kinky '60s patent-leather boots, stilettos recuperated from sex shops, bovver-boy and military boots. However, while punks elevated the ready-made, several notable street brands also curried favor. Some of the sharper vendors and manufacturers sussed that there might be a market opportunity in catering to these bizarre, new-wave exigencies.

A striking example is the famed Dr. Martens. Through the 1980s and beyond, the firm would create multiple variations of its 1960 classic, the eight-hole boot. Punks/DMs became synonymous as time went on.

Mid-seventies
Platform shoes, leopard print
Photo by kind permission of Nazim Mustafaev
Russian Virtual Shoe Museum

Dr. Martens
Photo by kind permission of
Nazim Mustafaev
Russian Virtual Shoe Museum

DR. MARTENS

At the beginning of the last century in Wollaston, Northamptonshire, the Griggs factory mainly manufactured pit boots for miners and army boots. Bulldog Boots were produced for the forces: the classic ten-eyelet military boot with hobnail sole and toe stitching (currently marketed as "Getta Grip"). In the fifties, Griggs bought the patent from German manufacturers Märtens and Funck, anglicized the name and started the brand Dr. Marten. On April 1st, 1960 the very first pair of "Docs" tread onto the UK market. This was the classic 8-hole DM, cherry-red (oxblood 1460, and still in production). From postal workers to factory workers, these were the preferred, practical choice: boots of the manly working class. When worn by skins, punks, and rude boys, DMs was an icon of their proletarian heritage and sense of belonging.

BROTHEL CREEPERS

Punks also enjoyed a dalliance with the British Brothel Creeper, a very different model of footwear. Designed in 1949 by George Cox Ltd. (an evergreen UK footwear company), they were originally marketed under the name "Hamilton."

These shoes sold well and generated a number of modelsand imitations. They appeared in many variations but always with flat soles made out of thick crepe-rubber (although thinner versions exist). There were several options for fastening: laces, typically with four D-rings; buckles; or a velcro closure. Teddy Boys went for flash leopard, tiger, or zebra-skin uppers, but creepers were also produced in a range of colors and materials, from shiny leather and suede to all-rubber and ersatz leather. They also came in many shapes, from the classic elongated tip to the more modern models with a rounded toe.

Brothel Creepers
Photos by kind permission of
Nazim Mustafaev
Russian Virtual Shoe Museum

WINKLEPICKERS

Winklepickers functioned as shoes, ankle boots, and deadly weapons, boasting an exaggeratedly pointed toe. They were worn by Teddy Boys strutting around in the sixties, and later recycled by punks and re-marketed using a variety of updated materials and design details.

SHELLY'S

Shelly's in the West End sold a pointed, black and white model. Its different look drew attention and thus gained traction in punk circles, and, later, with the mods revivalists, all thanks to The Jam.

SHELLY'S
of LONDON
533 OXFORD St. LONDON W1
MAKERS of ORIGINAL
TAM SHOES
ALL COLOURS
WHITE & PLATTED · BLACK & PLATTED
BLACK & WHITE · RED & WHITE
BROWN & BEIGE · GREEN & BEIGE
BEIGE & WHITE · BLUE & WHITE
BEIGE & BROWN · BEIGE & BEIGE
RED & BEIGE
Shoe 1
Shoe 2
Shoe 3
Just Send £12·99p Plus £1 Postage A PAIR
PLEASE STATE STYLE 1·2 OR 3 COLOUR AND YOUR ADRESS
THEY WILL BE SENT BY RETURN OF POST!!
BUY YOUR SHOES FROM THE FACTORY
SIZES FROM SIZE 3s IN BOYS TO SIZE 11s IN MENS
+ HALF SIZES ·

definitive lounge lizard-wear
buckle and thick crepe sole
Black patent leather.
Ladies sizes: 5-10
Mens sizes: 5-12
$ 62.95
364
FOOTWEAR FROM LONDON
6 buckles and zipper in front
Black leather.
Ladies sizes: 5-10
Mens sizes: 5-12
$ 65.95
21
787
#787 B&W creeper
two-tone with buckle
Ladies sizes: 5-10
Mens sizes: 5-12
$ 62.95
788
111
#111 Standard creeper
embellished version of the original
Creeper, with buckle and integrated
leather strip. Black leather.
Ladies sizes: 5-10
Mens sizes: 5-12
$ 62.95
#788 Suede creep
decorative side buckle
integrated leather strip
Black suede.
Ladies sizes: 5-10
Mens sizes: 5-12
$ 62.95
ALL OUR PRICES INCLUDE SHIPPING & HANDLING !!!
#47 JB4 half boot
laces up with 4 decorative buckles
Black suede.
Ladies sizes: 5-10
Mens sizes: 5-12
$ 64.95
47
#470 Round creeper
anti-pointy with side buckle
Black suede.
Ladies sizes: 5-10
Mens sizes: 5-12
$ 62.95
470
#144 Double buckle boot
very pointed and flat
2 buckles and frontal flap
Black leather.
Ladies sizes: 5-10
Mens sizes: 5-12
$ 59.95
144
IOGEY'S LTD. • P.O. BOX 8398 • LONG ISLAND CITY, NY 11101

VIVIENNE WESTWOOD

1980
Black leather shoes with laces and square toe
The Pirate collection
Photo by kind permission of Nazim Mustafaev
Russian Virtual Shoe Museum

1980, BOY, London
Photo by kind permission of
Nazim Mustafaev
Russian Virtual Shoe Museum

<
Vivienne Westwood
Lavender boots from Seditionaries
Photo by kind permission of
PunkPistol Collection

>>
05.1978, Richie Stott's cast-off boots
Plasmatics, end of gig
Paradise Rock Club, Boston
Photo Richard Parsons

Hood
100% PURE ORANGE JUICE
Hood
PUSH APART

ACC ESS RIES

ZIPS, SAFETY PINS AND RAZOR BLADES

TERENCE SELLERS
EDO BERTOGLIO
CHOKER RABBIT "R" PADLOCK
SID VICIOUS
MELODY MAKER
NART
EN ATTENDANT
PETER GRAVELLE
MEREDITH JACOBSON MARCIANO

FAKE AS FASHION?

LINDA STOKES
ANGUS COOK
DAVID GWINNUTT
M. WYNN
SLASH
JACKIE SHAPIRO
GEORGE DUBOSE
SHADES
SKUM
JIMMY JOCOY
HIGH TIMES
HELP

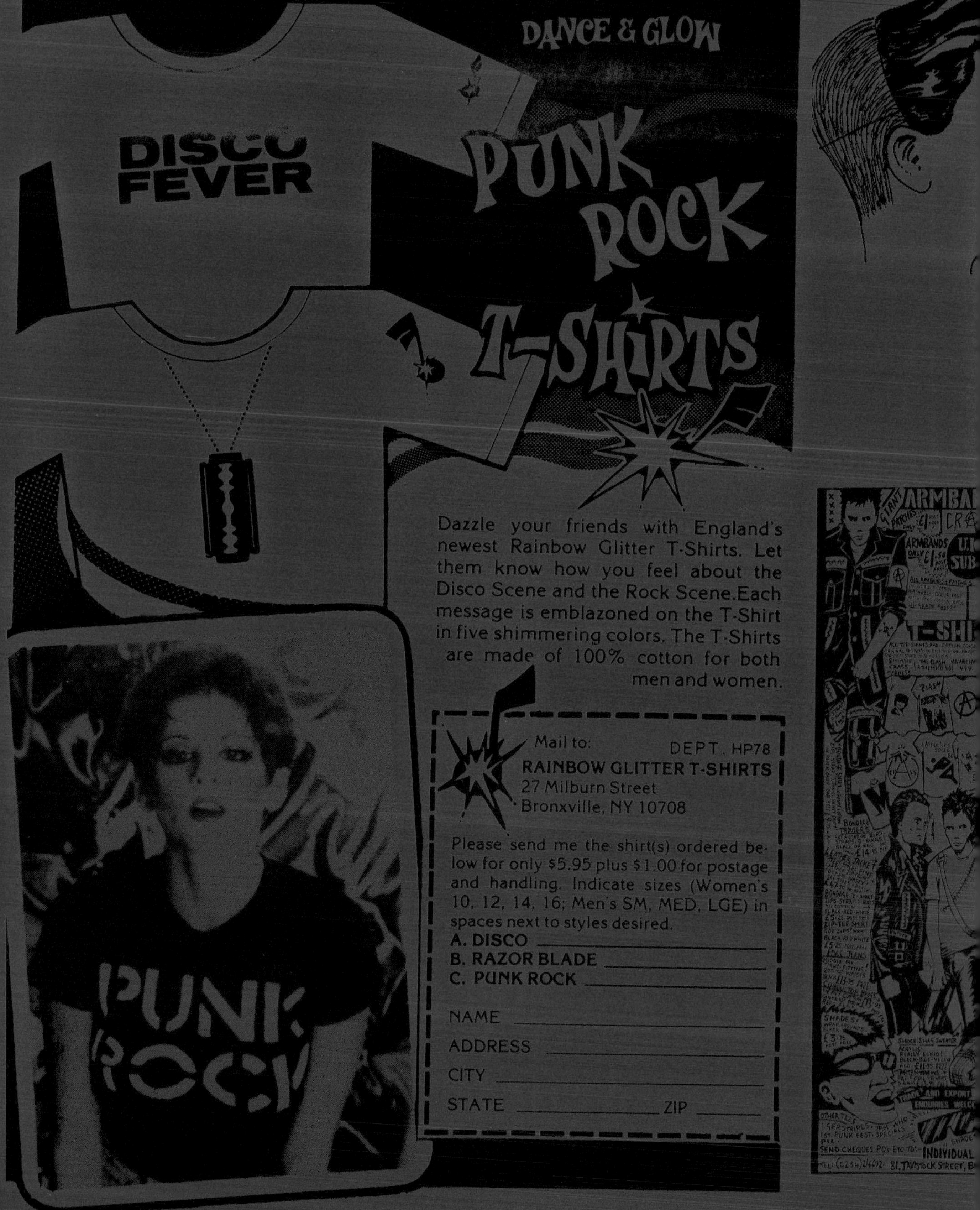

DANCE & GLOW
DISCO FEVER
PUNK ROCK T-SHIRTS
Dazzle your friends with England's newest Rainbow Glitter T-Shirts. Let them know how you feel about the Disco Scene and the Rock Scene. Each message is emblazoned on the T-Shirt in five shimmering colors. The T-Shirts are made of 100% cotton for both men and women.
Mail to: DEPT. HP78
RAINBOW GLITTER T-SHIRTS
27 Milburn Street
Bronxville, NY 10708
Please send me the shirt(s) ordered below for only $5.95 plus $1.00 for postage and handling. Indicate sizes (Women's 10, 12, 14, 16; Men's SM, MED, LGE) in spaces next to styles desired.
A. DISCO
B. RAZOR BLADE
C. PUNK ROCK
NAME
ADDRESS
CITY
STATE
ZIP
PUNK ROCK
ARMBA
T-SHI
INDIVIDUAL
81, TAVISTOCK STREET, B

This offer is not associated with or made by Warner Bros. Records Inc. or any affiliated company.

NTP 518 NEW TRADITIONALIST POMP – When the *circumstances* call for *pomp*, be ready with your "DEVO-DOO"; fabricated from durable A.B.S. plastic and designed with you in mind. (Basic black, one size fits all.)

EG 1248 ENERGY DOME – A special red vacu-form plastic hat designed and worn by DEVO in concert, on TV and in airports.

EZC 123 DEVO E-Z LISTENING CASSETTE – Muzak versions of your favorite DEVO tunes performed by DEVO at a *rare casual moment*. Mutated versions of DEVO classics, *Whip it*, *Mongoloid*, and many others round out this limited edition collecters item.

1979, Terence Sellers
New York
Photo Edo Bertoglio

ZIPS, SAFETY PINS AND RAZOR BLADES

HABERDASHERIES AND HARDWARE STORES WERE INEXHAUSTIBLE QUARRIES FOR TREASURE… FASTENERS MADE OF PLASTIC, LEATHERS, RHINESTONES, SEQUINS, AND ALL TYPES OF TRIMMINGS.

The punk belt was the most popular accessory. It was very in and could be decorated with anything: plastic tape, safety pins, chains of different shapes and styles that could be bought from hardware stores and used as neck chains or bracelets for wrists and ankles.

Borrow the studded leather collar from your cat or dog and strap it around your wrist, neck, ankle, or wherever it fits. Black with chrome studs is ideal for the bondage look. A luggage tag can be tied to the belt — write any name and your address, at least they'll know where to drop you off. It doesn't matter what kind of belt you wear — it's just critical you have one.

Look out for whips and chains (metal or plastic) and real tight, high-high stockings, red or black, for him and her, to turn your legs white like the inside of a radish. Give a Hitlerian touch to your haberdashery with Gestapo swastikas and SS skulls… less easy to find nowadays at flea markets, but just watch people's reaction!

A must accessory for both sexes is an unconventional old tie, worn over a T-shirt or thrown among other accessories or knotted in a loose, carefree fashion at the collarbone. Those obsolete bootlace ties from the fifties work perfectly; or rip a strip from a plastic shopping bag and, voilà, the tie is done.

The iconic Rabbit padlock
"Worn" by Sid Vicious

1978, Punks
Hollywood, CA
Photo Meredith Jacobson Marciano

Another tie (or necklace) trick, requires a chunky industrial zipper. Instructions: unzip and place around the neck (keeping the fastened end dangling at the front); wrap the loose ends around the back of the neck and join them with a safety pin. Hang safety pins and any other small knickknackery on the front slider tab. Now zip up your tie with teeth!

Add earrings? Safety-pins, badges or staples in the earlobes will do.

To allay any doubt, form the letters "P-U-N-K" with chains of tiddly safety pins fastened to a shirt or the back of a jacket. A bathroom plug and chain (or key-ring-like beads) can be slung around a torn T-shirt. Use safety pins to hold together the shreds; they're the emblems of punk rock, after all, so use them generously on tops and trousers, scattered or aligned like rows of sewn stitches.

09.1977, "Melody Makers"
Chunky bracelets
and ear medallions
(UK magazine)

>
"Nart" #1
Metal Clothing
(US fanzine)

METAL CLOTHING
FOR SELF PROTECTION
EFFICIENT IN DESIGN & FIT
SAM EDWARDS
415-431-7595

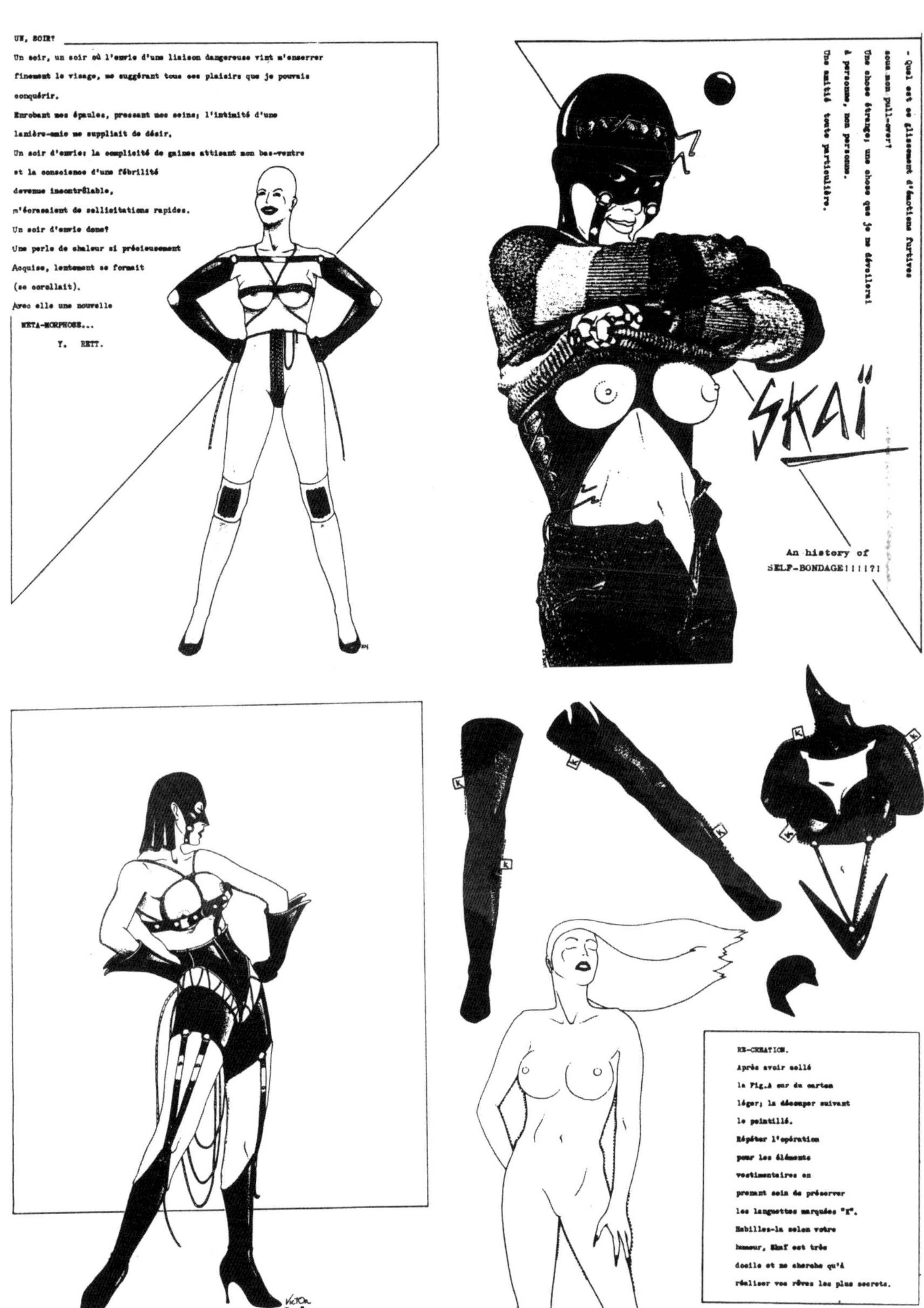

03.1978, "En attendant"
A history of self bondage

>
Fet
Photo Peter Gravelle

1982, Angus Cook
In a black mask
Regents Park, 1982
Photo David Gwinnutt

FAKE AS FASHION?

(OR, THE PRACTICAL/SOCIAL/AESTHETIC [I.E. PUNK] APPLICATION OF COSMETIC PROSTHETIC DEVICES)

"SO YOU AREN'T FAMILIAR WITH TODAY'S COSMETIC PROSTHETICS? WELL, READ ON...

MODERN MEDICAL TECHNOLOGY, SCIENTIFIC MECHANICS, AND ART HAVE BLENDED THEIR EXPERTISE TO BRING US LIFE-LIKE, TO THE TOUCH AND THE EYE, COSMETIC PROSTHETIC (FAKE) BODY PARTS...

...HAD YOU THOUGHT AT ALL ABOUT PUTTING THOSE INDUSTRIAL STAPLES AND SAFETY PINS THROUGH A PROSTHETIC INSTEAD OF YOUR REAL ONE? THE RESULTS ARE JUST AS STUNNING, AND CONSIDERING THE OBVIOUS ADVANTAGES, TWICE AS CHIC."

Linda Stokes

12.1977, "Slash"
Illustration M. Wynn
for FAKE AS FASHION?
(US fanzine)

07.1980, Jackie Shapiro's latex jewelry worn by models
New York
Photo George DuBose

"Skum" #4
Shades shop, London
Advert
(UK fanzine)

CHELSEA ANTIQUE MARKET, 352 KINGS RD. LONDON SW3

TROY HAS A LARGE SELECTION OF UNUSUAL SHADES

FOR A LARGE SELECTION OF UNUSUAL PEOPLE!

.VA WRAP - $10
›lack, red, purple, yellow

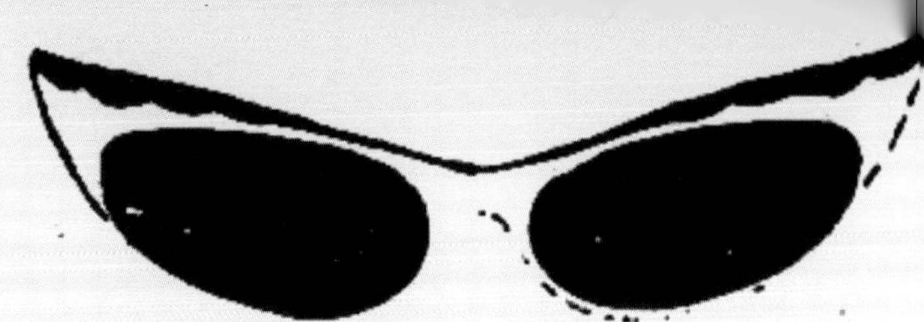

TIGRESS - $10
black, gold, silver, tortoise

SSIC WRAP - $10
lack (one piece, unhinged)

CLASSIC CAT - $10
black, white, tortoise
(with inset rhinestones - $13)

RAP - $10
k plastic and brass frames
or green lens

BAMBOO - $7

BLE WRAP - $7
lack

107 - $9
black, red, blue, purple, green, pink
(transparent colors)

hoices & mail to:

<
1976-1980, San Francisco
Photo Jimmy Jocoy

Fuck-Me Fashions

Le Look is fuck-you fashions that tell every-one "fuck me." Wet mouths, moist eyes, hot pants in cling-ing nylon ciré. Safety pins

TEE ITSE
OMA
PUNK-
PAITA!

Pekka Helos, teksti ja kuva

★ Rautaa ja kettinkiä, aaarghh! Villin vallankumouksen nuoret kapinalliset ovat tänään punk ja pukeutuvat myös sen mukaisesti.
★ Help! esittelee tässä jokaisen punkkarin paidanvalmistusohjeet.
★ Istu ja askartele!

● Punk on sitä, mitä kesy ei kestä, vanhus ei valitse eikä rauhallinen rakasta. Jos haluat olla mukana muodissa ja kauhuna koulussa, on korkea aika valmistaa oma punk-paita. Kaupasta niitä saa. Kehittele oma mallisi itse tai tutki tästä.
● Millainen on oikea punk-paita? Sen saat itse päättää, riittää kun siinä on tarpeeksi hakasia, ketjuja ja vetoketjuja. Hakaneula huulessa kuuluu asiaan, niin myös ketju korvaan. Jos aiot upottaa hakaneulan ihoosi, muista, ettei se tykkää hyvää tavallisesta metallista. Hopeinen hakaneula ei aiheuta tulehduksia korvan reijässä.
● Hyvä paita syntyy kimaltelevasta vuorisilkistä. Etupuolen on oltava sileä, taakse voit tehdä napeilla kiinnityksen. Paitaamme kului rahaa ja tavaraa seuraavasti:

60 cm vuorisilkkiä	[illegible]
2 vetoketjua	6.30 mk
niittejä	11.50 mk
kultanauhaa	16.75 mk
ketjua	0.00 mk
avainrenkaita	0.84 mk
lankaa	0.80 mk
Klubimestarin nappeja yms.	12.00 mk
	64.29 mk

20

09.1977, "Help"
"Make your punk shirt!"
text and image by Pekka Helos
60 cm lining in imitation silk, two zippers,
paper clips, golden braiding, key-ring chain,
yarn, various badges
(Finnish magazine)

<
03.1978, "High Times"
Fuck-Me Fashion
(US magazine)

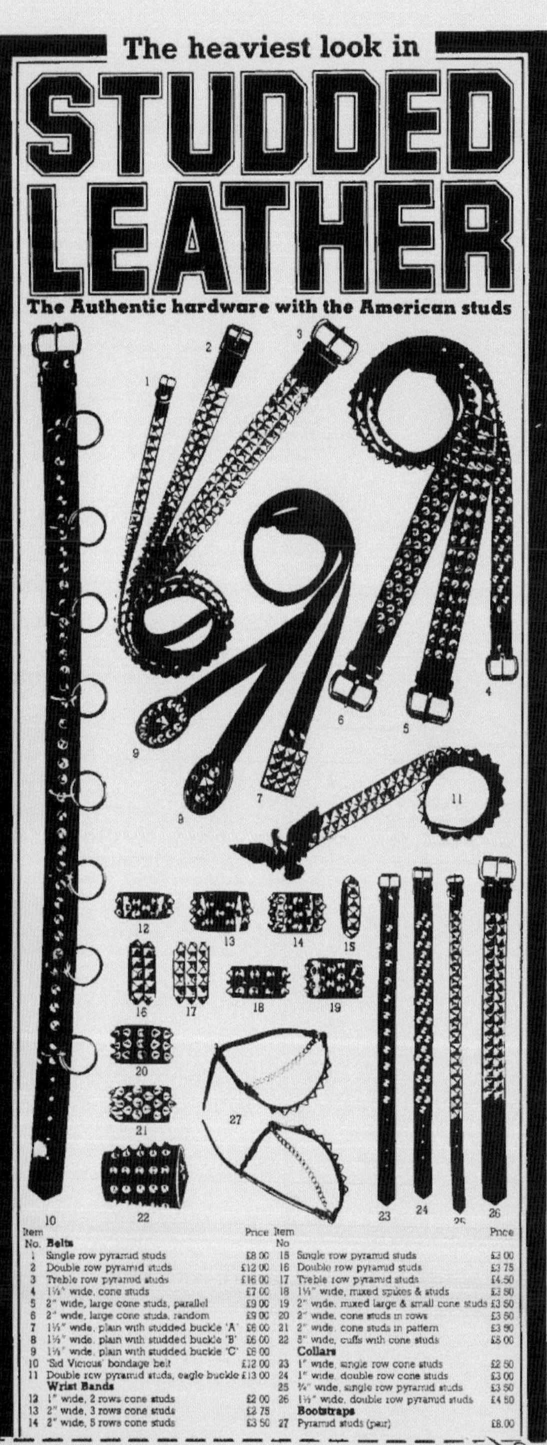

Item No.	Belts	Price	Item No		Price
1	Single row pyramid studs	£8.00	15	Single row pyramid studs	£3.00
2	Double row pyramid studs	£12.00	16	Double row pyramid studs	£3.75
3	Treble row pyramid studs	£16.00	17	Treble row pyramid studs	£4.50
4	1½" wide, cone studs	£7.00	18	1½" wide, mixed spikes & studs	£3.50
5	2" wide, large cone studs, parallel	£9.00	19	2" wide, mixed large & small cone studs	£3.50
6	2" wide, large cone studs, random	£9.00	20	2" wide, cone studs in rows	£3.50
7	1½" wide, plain with studded buckle 'A'	£6.00	21	2" wide, cone studs in pattern	£3.90
8	1½" wide, plain with studded buckle 'B'	£6.00	22	5" wide, cuffs with cone studs	£5.00
9	1½" wide, plain with studded buckle 'C'	£6.00		**Collars**	
10	'Sid Vicious' bondage belt	£12.00	23	1" wide, single row cone studs	£2.50
11	Double row pyramid studs, eagle buckle	£13.00	24	1" wide, double row cone studs	£3.00
	Wrist Bands		25	¾" wide, single row pyramid studs	£3.50
12	1" wide, 2 rows cone studs	£2.00	26	1½" wide, double row pyramid studs	£4.50
13	2" wide, 3 rows cone studs	£2.75		**Bootstraps**	
14	2" wide, 5 rows cone studs	£3.50	27	Pyramid studs (pair)	£6.00

ORDER FORM

Please send me item(s) no. . . . .

. . . .

My wrist size is . . . . . . inches

My belt size is . . . . . . inches

I enclose cheque/Postal order for £ . . . . . .

(Note: Add 50p for Post & Packing)

NAME . . . .

ADDRESS . . . .

. . . .

Send your order to:-

The Rock Art Shop
34 Old Compton Street
London W.1.

or

Call in the shop and see us where we also stock London's largest selection of T-shirts, crazy colour hair dye, coloured hair sprays, posters, badges, jewellery etc.

(All orders despatched within 10 days)

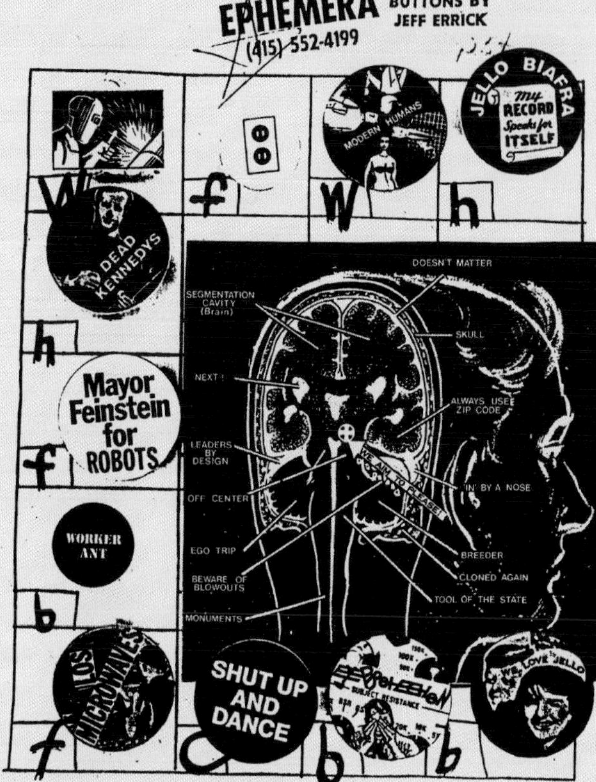

er, brass studdied 2½ inches wide
duty clasps. Real machismo! **Only**
o for £3)
WRIST BANDS Have your name,
roup or slogan punched onto it. No
same quality and same price (two
ve one studdied and one printed!
LAR WRIST BANDS 18 inch long

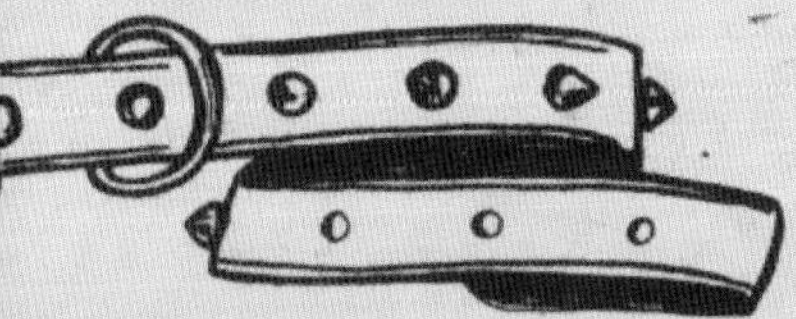

rap with brass buckle and studs
led around the wrist. Only for hard
s! £1.50
ETAL WRIST BANDS Cast out of
s (3oz) nice 'n' chunky only **£1.75**
e giving away a £4 record
for the most original or
order we receive each week
and Packing is free in the UK
service get it straight from
SEAGULL TRADING CO.
inus Road, Eastbourne Sussex
E. for free leather goods catalogue

Brass studded, real machismo punk style, 2½" wide with heavy duty press studs. **Only £1.65.**
Printed wrist bands. Have your name, favourite group or slogan punched onto it. Up to 12 letters — no studs, but same quality and same price.
Also **Heavy metal wrist bands**, cast out of solid brass. Nice 'n' chunky, only **£1.75**
Fast service, get it straight from:
SEAGULL TRADING COMPANY
9 TERMINUS ROAD, EASTBOURNE, SUSSEX

ELECTRONIC BADGES!!!

Astonish delight bewilder or just BORE everybody with this latest line in badges (size 1½" x 1"). Each badge contains a tiny light emitting diode and flashes a red light when the badge pin is closed.

100 Hours continuous Flashing ***12 Month Guarentee*** ***Free Battery*** ***Scratch Resistant*** ***Fluorescent Colours***

All this for only £3.75 each including p&p & free battery

Send to INDIVIDUAL TRADING CO
Dept SH 81 Tavistock St
Bedford MK40 2RR. Tel (0234) 216692

TWO-TONE BELTS

CHECK

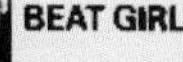

BEAT GIRL

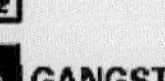

SKA

GANGSTER DANCING

MADNESS 'M'

SPECIALS FACE

Send **£1.50** (Cheque or P.O.) (P&P incl.) to **BADGE SALES** 48 Carnaby Street, W1.
Wholesale enquiries welcome.

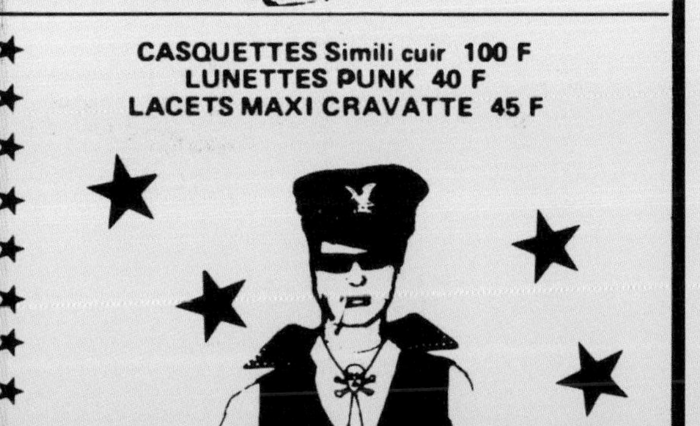

SHO
PPI
NG

SHOPPING

BOY
SEDITIONARIES
ACME SUR
KITSCH-22
SMUTZ
MANIC PANIC
IAN'S
TRASH AND VAUDEVILLE
REVENGE
NEXT EMPIRE
CHICKEN LITTLE
GRANNY'S OF LONDON
POSEUR
ZIPPERHEAD
EDDIE KENT
CREAM SODA
EDWIGE
EDO BERTOGLIO
RECORD MIRROR
MASAYOSHI SUKITA

SEDITIONARIES
LONDON

VIVIENNE WESTWOOD
NO FUTURE
JOHN SAVAGE
THE FACE
DAVID CONNOR
SCHOOL FOR WIVES
ALEXANDER TROCCHI
MICKYE MOUSE
BELSTAFF
JOHNNY ROTTEN
SEX PISTOLS
PUNKPISTOL COLLECTION
MALCOLM MCLAREN
LET IT ROCK
TACKY FANZINE
BROMLEY CONTINGENT
SIOUXSIE SIOUX
JORDAN
SIMON 'BOY' BARKER
DEBBIE JUVENILE WILSON
LINDA ASHBY
PHILIP SALON
SIMONE THOMAS
BERTIE 'BERLIN' MARSHALL
TRACIE O'KEEFE
STEVE SEVERIN
BILLY IDOL
SHARON HAYMAN

KITSCH-22
LONDON

WENDY MAY
JAN HORROX
MODZART
TERRY DE HAVILLAND
ANDY SOTIRIOU
JOHN DOVE
MOLLY WHITE
CATCH-22
JOSEPH HELLER
BEATLES
BOY
BLACKMAIL
KITSCH-22

BOY
LONDON

JOHN KREVINE
STEPHANE RAYNOR
ACME ATTRACTION
PX
TIT-BITS
BOY BLACKMAIL
XEROX
DEREK HUTCHINS
SHEILA ROCK
ANDY SOTIRIOU
GARY GILMORE
GENESIS P-ORRIDGE
PROSTITUTION
INSTITUTE OF CONTEMPORARY ARTS
KITSCH-22
MODZART
SEDITIONARIES
BOGEY NY
FLASH PUBLISHING

POSEUR
LOS ANGELES

JIM O'CONNOR
VOGUE
QUEEN
CLUB MAGAZINE
NOVA
MEREDITH JACOBSON MARCIANO
STUFF
CARRON
PAMLA MOTOWN

MANIC PANIC
NEW YORK

TISH BELLOMO
EILEEN BELLOMO (AKA SNOOKY)
GLENN BROWN
DOWNTOWN 81
RAMONES
BLONDIE
CBGB
MAX'S KANSAS CITY
DROP-OUTS
RUSSELL WOLINSKY
SIC F*CKS
SNOOKY

TRASH & VAUDEVILLE
NEW YORK

JIMMY WEBB
RAY GOODMAN
PUNK
BEATLES
PATTI SMITH
IGGY POP
RAMONES
BLONDIE
HEARTBREAKERS
DEAD BOYS
NEW YORK ROCKER
TOM WHITE
UNNATURAL AXE
RICHARD PARSONS

REVENGE
NEW YORK

JOSEPH TOMASELLO
TERRY JONES
CBGB'S
CHERYL
DEBBIE
EILEEN
PRETTY PRETTY PUNK PAM
RICHARD PARSONS
NATASHA
BARBARA
ACE
TRIXIE

EDDIE KENT
BOSTON

SUBWAY NEWS
HIGH SOCIETY
FASHION TO BOOT
GARMENT DISTRICT

ZIPPERHEAD
PHILADELPHIA

DEAD MILKMEN
RICK MILLAN
RAYMOND ERCOLI
CLEOPATRA
LIZ TAYLOR
BOY
VIVIENNE WESTWOOD
FIORUCCI

1979, Edwige
Photo Edo Bertoglio

>
01.1977, "Record Mirror"
Punk calendar
(UK music paper)

SHOPPING

For your complete punk wardrobe, just visit London's BOY, Seditionaries, Acme Sur, Kitsch-22, Smutz; New York's Manic Panic, Ian's, Trash & Vaudeville, Revenge, Next Empire; San Francisco's Chicken Little; Los Angeles's Granny's of London's outlet, Poseur; Philadelphia's Zipperhead; Boston's Eddie Kent; Tokyo's Cream Soda.

These were punk's embryonic nuclei around the world, but between the late-seventies and earlyeighties the diffusion of the new wave became truly global. In addition to the aforementioned stores, fresh outlets sprang up in peripheral towns across the States, Canada, Britain, and in various European capitals, while a new tide of designers engulfed the market.

1977, Seditionaries
London
Photo Masayoshi Sukita

SEDITIONARIES, LONDON

"WE JUST CAME UP WITH MORE AND MORE SEXUAL IMAGERY ON OUR T-SHIRTS AND BEGAN TO SEE THE PERTINENCE OF IT.
THE FACT IS THAT IF YOU REALLY DO WANT TO FIND OUT HOW MUCH FREEDOM YOU HAVE IN THIS BRITISH SOCIETY AT THE MOMENT, THE BEST WAY IS JUST TO MAKE AN OVERT SEXUAL STATEMENT AND YOU'LL HAVE ALL THE HOUNDS OF HELL ON YOUR BACK. CERTAINLY IN THIS COUNTRY ITS THE THING THAT BRINGS OUT EVERYONE'S EMOTIONAL PREJUDICES, SO MUCH SO THAT BY THE TIME THEY'VE FINISHED THEY ARE REALLY QUITE LUNATIC. SO, WE BEGAN TO THINK ABOUT SEXUAL CLOTHING AND MATERIALS LIKE RUBBER TO MAKE PEOPLE MUCH MORE AWARE OF THEIR BODIES AND TO FLAUNT THEMSELVES, IN ORDER TO CONFRONT PEOPLE. A YOUNG GIRL WEARING A RUBBER SKIRT TO THE OFFICE IS GOING TO PRODUCE A REACTION. THAT'S WHAT CLOTHES ARE ALL ABOUT AND THAT'S WHY PEOPLE WEAR THEM. YOU CAN'T WALK DOWN THE STREET IN ANYTHING I'VE EVER MADE AND NOT GET A STARE."

Vivienne Westwood
(Interviewed in No Future fanzine 1977)

Vivienne Westwood
Tits T-Shirt

>
Vivienne Westwood
Clothing label: for soldiers
prostitutes
dykes + punks

for
soldiers
prosti-
tutes
dykes+
punks

Seditionaries was London's first cutting-edge punk shop, which made possible "the only modern look of the seventies," as quipped John Savage in *The Face*. Designed in collaboration with David Connor, the interior design of the shop was an aesthetic amplification of that period's street style. The interior walls were overlaid with blown-up photos of bombed-out Dresden, flanked by an upside-down Piccadilly Circus.

The shoes, fabrics, T-shirts, and trousers sold in the shop were extravagant and outrageous, inspired by bikers, fetishists, and prostitutes. The projects that came out of that boutique/laboratory played around with sexuality and other taboos; printed T-shirts with the Cambridge Rapist's hood, semi-naked cowboys, exposed breasts, pornographic phrases from Alexander Trocchi's book School for Wives, swastikas, and Micky Mouse porn...

Vivienne Westwood
Seditionaries
Black Bondage suit

Vivienne Westwood
Seditionaries shirt
"Only Anarchists are pretty"
Photo by kind permission of
PunkPistol Collection

A typical Seditionaries artifact was the muslin longsleeved top: simply two squares of fabric with elongated sleeves, similar to a straitjacket, held together with D-rings. The most notorious iteration of this was the Destroy T-shirt, complete with a swastika and inverted crucifix.

The Bondage suit was another mainstay, which emerged in 1976: a cross between a US military jumpsuit and the buckled-up Belstaff motorcycle jacket. A black fabric version was first aired by Johnny Rotten in Paris, causing quite a stir. The pants had a zipper under the crotch with a detachable flap, ankle straps, and even a kind of built-in thong. A Scottish tartan variant, among others, would also be produced.

Vivienne Westwood
Seditionaries
Tartan Bondage suit
Photo by kind permission
of PunkPistol Collection

All Seditionaries' clothes had been designed by Vivienne Westwood with input from Malcolm McLaren, an unbroken partnership from the days of Let It Rock in 1972. Production was underpinned by sundry external collaborators who actually crafted the garments; part-time seamstresses and old ladies who knitted mohair sweaters. Nothing was factory-made, which is why quality of the handiwork lacked consistency.

Vivienne Westwood
Seditionaries Bondage Jacket
Photo by kind permission of
PunkPistol Collection

SEX

Vivienne Westwood
Seditionaries
Safety Pin Queen Muslin
Photo by kind permission of
PunkPistol Collection

>
Seditionaries
Flyer
Private collection

THE IDEA WAS TO TAKE THE WEARING OF FETISH GEAR "OUT OF THE BEDROOM AND INTO THE STREETS." FOR WESTWOOD, SARTORIAL SEDITIONS WERE POLITICAL WEAPONS, PROMPTING REVOLUTIONARY ACTS AGAINST A STAID SOCIAL SYSTEM:

"BECAUSE WE'VE ALWAYS TRIED TO CONFRONT PEOPLE TO FIND OUT [THEIR ISSUES] AND BEEN CONCERNED WITH CHANGING THINGS, GIVING PEOPLE THE CONFIDENCE TO ASSERT THEMSELVES AS THEY REALLY ARE. IT'S JUST POLARIZED INTO A MORE DEFINITE POLITICAL CONCEPT NOW. SEDITION TO US MEANS TO SEDUCE PEOPLE INTO REVOLT AND THAT'S WHAT WE'RE TRYING TO DO."

Vivienne Westwood, *Tacky Fanzine*

Regular clients (some also shop assistants) were known as "The Bromley Contingent," a cluster of Pistols friends and followers, including. Linda Ashby, Simon 'Boy' Barker, Sharon Hayman, Billy Idol, Debbie Juvenile, Jordan, Tracie O'Keefe, Bertie 'Berlin' Marshall, Philip Salon, Steve Severin, Siouxsie Sioux, Simone Thomas.

Sedition

Conduct or speech inciting people to rebel against the authority of a state or monarch.

Origin: late Middle English (in the sense of 'violent strife');

from Old French, or from Latin *seditio(n-)*,

from *sed-* 'apart' + *itio(n-)* 'going' (from the verb *ire*).

SEX original
DANCE
'ello Joe been anywhere lately
Nah its all played aht, Bill
Gettin too straight.

Vivienne Westwood
Seditionaries
Mickey Mouse Fucking Minnie Mouse (shirt)
Photo by kind permission of
PunkPistol Collection

>
Vivienne Westwood
Seditionaries
Be Reasonable Demand The Impossible (shirt)
Photo by kind permission of
PunkPistol Collection

<
Vivienne Westwood
Cowboys T-shirt (Sex original)
Photo by kind permission of
PunkPistol Collection

1977, Kitsch-22
Model Wendy May
Jumper Jan Horrox
Jeans Modzart
Boots Terry de Havilland
Photo Andy Sotiriou

>
1977, Kitsch-22
External shop sign
Photo Andy Sotiriou

KITSCH-22, LONDON

UNIQUE CLOTHING FOR BORED TEENAGERS AND OTHER FRUSTRATED OPTIMISTS

In 1976, John Dove and Molly White opened Kitsch-22 at number 22 Woodstock Street, London. They ought to be regarded as among the anticipators of punk culture and street fashion. They were undoubtedly pioneers in the sphere of graphic T-shirts as a fashion item.

Obviously the shop's name comes from the address, but it was also a nod to Joseph Heller's *Catch-22*. Published in 1961, the book was intended to be a fierce critique of obdurate military structures, revealed through the adventures of a group of US airmen were assigned a tally of bombing missions over Italy during World War II. The rules to which the aviators were subjected contained a bureaucratic absurdity, epitomized by regulation 22: whoever is crazy can ask to be exempted from flight missions, but those who ask to be exempted from flight missions are patently not crazy.

1978, Kitsch-22
Shop interior
Model Mike
Clothes Modzart
Photo Andy Sotiriou

>
1978, Kitsch-22
Model Wendy May
Clothes Modzart
Photo Andy Sotiriou

Kitsch-22 stocked modern art T-shirts, studded belts, fluorescent socks, electric-blue Fab-Four-style boots, camouflage trousers, pink leopard-skin jeans, flamingred mohair sweaters, as well as their Modzart printed jeans.

The success of Kitsch-22 clothing sales would soon lead to the closure of the tiny shop and the expansion of its operations into other retail outlets and be able to cope with an increasingly outspread demand. Eventually the brand's management engaged in international distribution.

In 1979, it partnered with BOY, offering a collection of screen-printed sweaters and Modzart trousers in catalog *Blackmail*.

4 Modzart Striped Jeans
6 Modzart Leopard Jeans
Design by *Kitsch-22*,
John Dove, Molly White
Boy Blackmail, first edition 1980
Printed by London Bridge Printing
by kind permission

2. Bongade Trousers
16. Nigel Shirt
18. Inspector Jacket
23. Floureshent Socks
30. Mickey Mouse T-Shirt
33. Sid Shirt
Design by *Kitsch-22*,
John Dove, Molly White
Boy Blackmail, first edition 1980
Printed by London Bridge Printing
by kind permission
of Mark Ciaramella archive

THE ALTERN

BONDAGE TROUSERS...

BLACK TIGHT FITTING BONDAGE JEANS - PATCH POCKETS, ZIP POCKETS D-RINGS LEG STRAPS

NOTE: THESE ARE THE ORIGINAL DESIGN

STATE WAIST SIZE ONLY AVAILABLE IN BLACK DRILL

ONLY - £15.95 + £1 PP

SLEEVELESS TIGER TEES

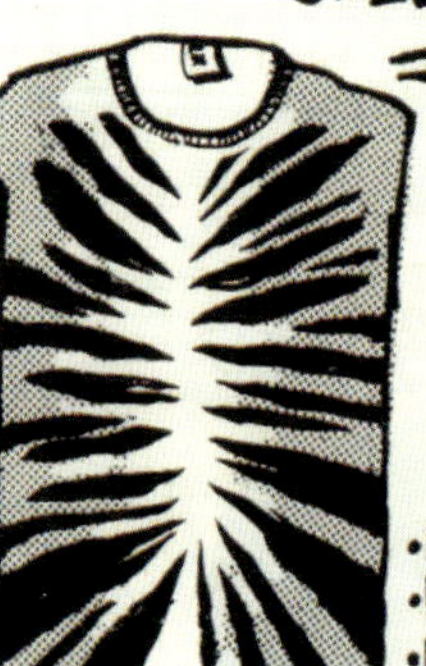

ALL OVER STRONG BLACK SKIN PATTERN ON SLEEVELESS WHITE TEESHIRT ON THE FOLLOWING BRIGHTLY COLOURED BACKGROUNDS

- BLACK ON BLUE
- BLACK ON ORANGE
- BLACK ON PINK
- BLACK ON YELLOW
- BLACK ON GREEN

SMALL / MED / LARGE

ONLY - £4.95 + 35p PP

BONDAGE JA

BLACK HEA
DUTY CLOTH J
AIRCRAFT T
TO DOG CLIPS
ACROSS YOU
STATE CHEST S

ACME BUMFLAPS →

'THE BETTER CLASS OF NAPPY' FOR BONDAGE TROUSERS, BACKED IN BLACKDRILL 14" ACROSS AND 10" DEEP WITH DOG CLIPS TO FIX TO ANYTHING

1. **LEOPARD FUR.**
2. **TARTAN** (RED)

£2.95 + 20p PP

NEW

BARBED WIRE

BRAND NEW DESIGN BIG-BIG
BARBED WIRE PRINT IN BLACK
WITH BLOOD RED DRIPS AND S
FRONT + BACK ON A GOOD Q
SLEEVELESS TEE (STATE SI

- £4.95 + 3 PP

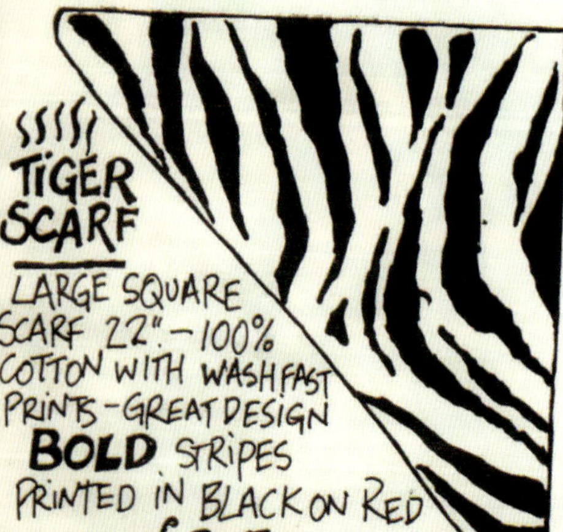

TIGER SCARF

LARGE SQUARE SCARF 22" - 100% COTTON WITH WASHFAST PRINTS - GREAT DESIGN **BOLD** STRIPES PRINTED IN BLACK ON RED

£2.50 + 20p PP

BONDAGE SHIRT-

QUALITY BLACK SHIRT WITH BLACK + RED ANARCHY PATCH ON SHOULDER + SHATTERED UNION JACK PATCH IN BLUE + RED - SIX STRAPS FROM THE SLEEVES TO THE POCKETS - A CLASSIC REBEL SHIRT ONLY - £11.95 + 60p PP

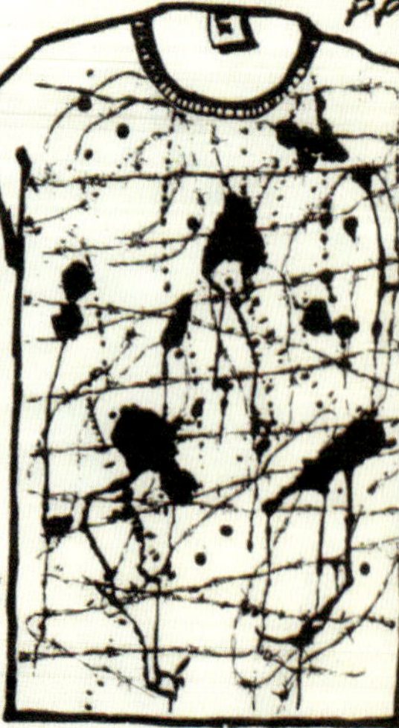

ATIVE
REMEMBER '76 - ALL OVER COLLAGE OF PISTOLS, CLASH, 999, SUZY CLIPS' FRONT + BACK ON A SPRAYED ORANGE SLEEVELESS TEE-SHIRT STATE SML £4.95 + 30p P+P.
999
VITH AN
RNESS CLIPPED
NT. AND STRAPS
ZIPS ETC...
£14.95 + £1 PP
STRAPS - STRAPS - STRAPS! - ON YOUR SHIRTS OR ON YOUR TROUSERS - BONDAGE STRAPS IN BLACK, WHITE, KHAKI. TWO DOG CLIPS - 'D' RINGS AND STRONG WEBBING - APPROX 1 METRE LONG
ONLY 75p + 25p P+P.
ZIPP-TEES.
BLACK TEE-SHIRT WITH "EIGHT" CHUNKY ZIPS. TO REVEAL THOSE INTERESTING PARTS OF THE ANATOMY!
DONT BE UNDONE ZIP UP NOW!!!
ONLY: £8.95 + 60p P+P
IN SMALL - MEDIUM - LARGE
RD TOPS
SPOT PRINT ON BRITE
D BACKGROUND ON
EESHIRTS THE SLEEVES
EN CUT OFF WHY PAY
HE PRICE WHEN OURS
TER — AND COST JUST:
N PINK
N GREEN
N YELLOW
N BLUE
STATE BUST / CHEST SIZE (S.M.L.) £4.95 + 35p PP

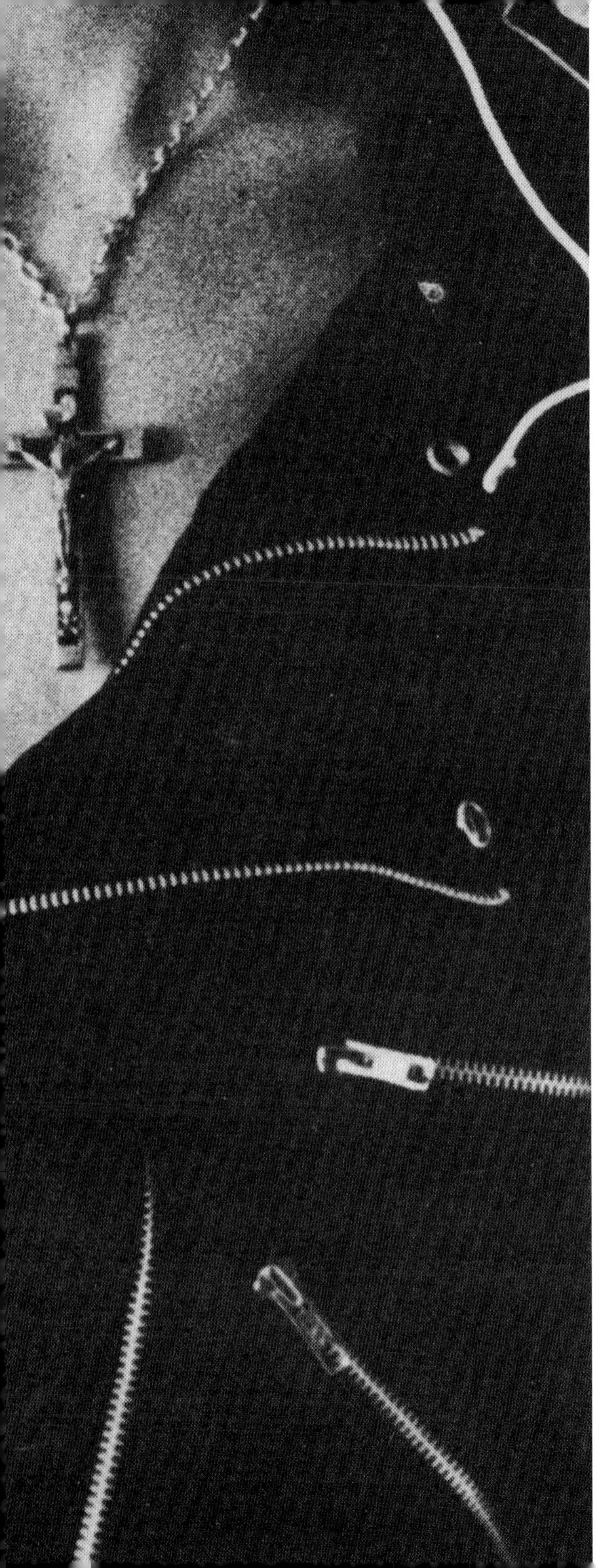

2. Bondage Trousers
18. Inspector Jacket
Design by *Kitsch-22*,
John Dove, Molly White
Boy Blackmail, first edition 1980
Printed by London Bridge Printing
by kind permission
of Mark Ciaramella archive

The charred remains of the mysterious arsonist displayed in BOY's window
Boy Blackmail, first edition 1980
Printed by London Bridge Printing
by kind permission
of Mark Ciaramella archive

BOY, LONDON

"WE'RE HERE TO MAKE MONEY. WE DO THAT, AS WE'VE ALWAYS DONE BY BEING DIFFERENT. THE BOYS LIKE OUR TOUCHES OF REALISM. THAT'S WHAT WE'RE SELLING—REALITY. IF YOU WANT A PRISSY ATMOSPHERE, DON'T COME HERE. GO SOMEWHERE ELSE TO BUY YOUR PATCHWORK JEANS."

John Krevine

Acme Attraction was the initial guise of Stephane Raynor and John Krevine's clothing store hangout in 1976. Then, in March 1977, 153 King's Road transformed itself into BOY under Krevine's direction, while Stephane Raynor and his girlfriend devoted their energies to PX, an early clothing store/workshop for new romantics in James Street, Covent Garden. In BOY's window display, there was a left foot, a finger, and some fragments of human skin: the remains of an imaginary arsonist, "killed" for having tried to set fire to the shop, and a advance warning for potential "imitators."

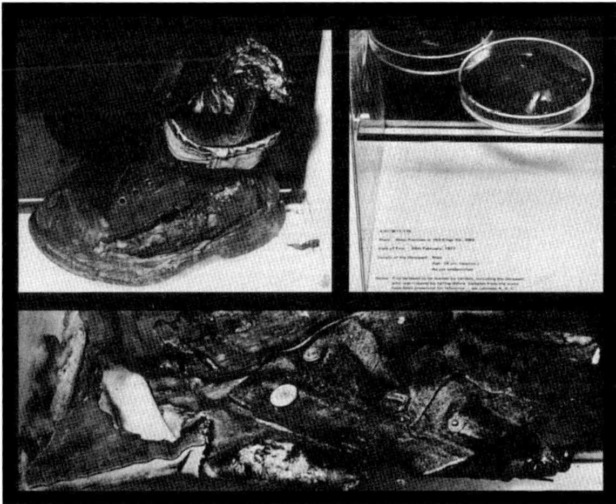

But after two days, following local complaints, the police raided and confiscated the "decorations." The owners were fined for "Indecent Exhibition" (*Act of Vagrancy 1824 - for the Punishment of idle and disorderly Persons, and Rogues and Vagabonds*).

Despite such setbacks, BOY succeded in propelling punk culture to the forefront of the public's attention. It was so successful that two more subsidiaries opened in London's Soho: one in Carnaby Street, one in Moor Street. Despite repeated attempts to shut it down, BOY remains open to this day. Mag-rag *Tit-Bits* ran a hit piece on the subject in April 1977:

"The latest bit of tat to open up in London's increasingly tatty King's Road is the brainchild of 28-year-old business adventurer John Krevine and friends. And it's a very sick idea. It's an insult even to call the place a boutique—it's a bizarre rubbish bin of sick, macabre clothes surrounded by wall-to-wall violence. The shop is called Boy and inside there are framed photographs of boys splattered along one wall. Boys... bloody, bruised and beaten up.

'It's realism,' said the quietly-spoken, clean-shaven Krevine who smiles gently as he flogs you a 'hate suit' or a pair of steel-capped boots. He is laughing softly at you, all the way to the nearest bank...

T-shirt Gary Gilmore Lives
Concept Genesis P-Orridge
Boy Blackmail, first edition 1980
Printed by London Bridge Printing
by kind permission of Mark Ciaramella archive

T-shirt Gary Gilmore Lives
Concept Genesis P-Orridge
(Private collection)

...Krevine denies he is trading in violence. Yet he relies on the gruesome to entice the young and curious to buy his hideous garb.
The grim publicity poster which landed on my desk showed a bloody and battered youth lying on the ground surrounded by booted legs and a clenched fist. [...] That might shock you, but by the time you reach the charred remains at the back of the shop you'll be punch drunk with the violence of it all. From brutal pictures to jewellery made of hypodermic Syringes and ugly straitjackets. [...]
If you're used to freaky boutiques with dim lights and funky music, you'll certainly find Boy different. There isn't any music for a start—I suppose if there were, the Funeral March would be most appropriate.
[...] Bitchy? It's the feeling of death and destruction around that prompted me! Death in the form of a wall of framed newspaper cuttings relating death and violence to young people. The boy executed in a cemetery... the boy who drowned... the one killed by a train... the boy hostage—and plain ordinary death by misadventure. They're all there."

In 1979 John Krevine met John Dove and Molly White of Kitsch-22 to consider a merger with BOY. They resolved to publish a curious mail-order catalog, a truly inimitable concept for the design and sale of BOY and Kitsch-22 originals. Krevine would fund the printing while Dove & White set up Flash Publishing, a publishing house to produce it. It rolled off 600 copies of the first BOY *Blackmail* catalog.

The style of BOY's catalog was that of a fanzine, interspersed with a smattering of color, eye-catching graphics, and photos by Derek Hutchins, Sheila Rock, and Andy Sotiriou.

One of the indelible lures of the shop was its "Gary Gilmour Lives" T-shirt, which a depicted the recent execution by firing squad in Utah State Prison of the aforementioned Gilmour, convicted of murder. It should come as no surprise that it was designed by Genesis P-Orridge, who had already scandalized the nation with *Prostitution,* an exhibition at the ICA. Other T-shirts hung around, some with fake animal blood, decorated with tubes and hospital bandages, some with slogans that were anti-marriage, anti-parent, anti-adult. They mingled with earrings made of contraceptive packaging and razor blades. In addition to the official BOY stock, Kitsch-22 garments were sold, followed by Modzart trousers with printed fabrics in fifty different varieties.

Soldiering on, into the eighties, BOY became the official reseller for Seditionaries' merchandise.

3. Baggy Bondage
16. Nigel Shirt
17. Wraparound shades
Design by *Kitsch-22*
John Dove, Molly White
Boy Blackmail, first edition 1980
Printed by London Bridge Printing
by kind permission of
Mark Ciaramella archive

POSEUR, LOS ANGELES

CLOTHES FOR THE MODERN WORLD

British émigré Jim O'Connor began designing and manufacturing clothes and footwear in the early seventies, achieving some early success in the UK thanks to articles in *Vogue*, *Queen*, *Club Magazine* and *Nova*. In 1976, he moved to the US and began employing the name "Poseur" for his clothing/fashion fanzine.

On his website, O'Connor recounts: "I was living in New York in 1976, designing and making clothing, and extremely dissatisfied with both the garment industry and with fashion journalism."

Poseur incorporated experimental graphics and was inspired by British punk fanzines. The first issues came out between 1976–77. Jim continues: "I had been reading some accounts of the punk scene as written by various journalists whom I call 'voyeurs.' These invisible writers all dismissed the kids who were at punk events as being no more than 'poseurs.' They said that the kids had got the idea of punk all wrong when they dressed up and posed. This voyeur viewpoint was saying that it is phony and pretentious to be interested in one's own clothing and appearance.

However, it seemed obvious to me that these 'poseurs' were my kindred spirit and that they knew, as well as I knew, that it is quite the reverse! – One of the basic points of punk was that in fact it is great fun to dress up and pose."

1979, Jim O'Connor al Poseur Shop
Los Angeles
Photo Meredith Jacobson Marciano

>
1978, "Stuff" #3
Poseur publicity
Hollywood, Los Angeles
(US fanzine)

POSEUR
7154 SUNSET : one block west of La Brea : 851-5919
LEFT
Hand knitted, wool jacket.
Many designs in stock
Black nylon ciré pants
Inspiration : MONDRIAN - POLLOCK - LICHTENSTEIN
Poseur : HOLLY
Hair & Makeup : RICHARD SHARRAH
Clothes : PAM & JIM
Artist
ABOVE
5-color print
cotton t-shirt
Concept : PAMLA MOTOWN
Fotos : JIM O'CONNOR
LEFT
Dayglo - pink & black
print on white
interlock
shirt & pants

1979, Poseur
Los Angeles
Photo Meredith Jacobson Marciano

Thanks to O'Connor's innate passion for clothing and disguise, *Poseur* quickly transmuted from a simple concept into a retail outlet in his Sunset Boulevard apartment in Hollywood. By the early eighties, the shop established itself on Melrose Avenue, which was, at that time, still a street of offices and furniture stores — but that was about to change.

O'Connor sold imported T-shirts and accessories from the UK. The shop's interior was awash with bright colors: the walls had randomly printed motifs in orange, yellow, and green. Hanging in bulk throughout the store were studded punk garb and ska togs in black and white. Glass showcases abounded, filled with jewelry, leather accessories, and a host of badges.

As O'Connor describes, "I've enjoyed dressing up and putting on a pose for as long as I can remember. Being in the company of others who are wearing interesting clothing has always been desirable to me. Having good music is important for a nice atmosphere when I venture into public places, but the main purpose of any public gathering is to see and be seen. So I realized that the word poseur fitted me well, and now I had a name for my main passion in life."

(Quote from O'Connor's official site: www.poseur.net)

1979, Poseur's Catalog
Los Angeles
Private collection

1979, Carron inside Poseur
Los Angeles
Photo Meredith Jacobson Marciano

BOTH THESE SHIRTS ARE MADE OF STRETCH TERRYCLOTH.
Price....$16.00
ZIPPER SHIRT
This shirt is infested with heavy black zippers, 4 in front,2 on the back All open to reveal bare bod beneath.
BLACK....# ZTA
RED......# ZTB
PURPLE...# ZTC
BLUE.....# ZTD
Price...$16.00
BONDAGE SHIRT
This one has a heavy black zipper in front which unzips to show bare chest.4 black loops with D rings at sides & & shoulders, + 2 detatchable

TELL ALL YOUR
FRIENDS ABOUT
Poseur

an interview with Jim O'Conner and Pamla Motown

Jim: "Well, the store was germinating in our minds about 10-15 years ago and it's been that long in the making. We started a year ago but it's something we've wanted to do for a long time."

Pam: We left art school in the mid 60's in London, and there were lots of boutiques, and that first sort of made us want to have one of our own."

Jim: "Particularly because we think the boutique is a good way to communicate directly with new clothes. We've learned in the years we've worked in the garment industry that clothes often get stopped in the process of being made and don't get marketed properly and never fully get released to the public, and that's what we're trying to do, is just make a variety of them available that wouldn't normally be accepted in the industry. To prove to ourselves and others that they're sellable and wearable. We would never suggest that it's a 60's thing, for us it's a continuation of something that started as long ago as the 60's when we were first at art college. I think we're trying to prove a point as well which is thiat - this is something that was killed off artificially, the bright colors, just the sort of variety of clothing, the sort of non formality of the clothing was something that as we worked andxf we found that people around us were not making these clothes anymore and were goingback to a style that was to us dated before we even got started in the business. We're trying to sort of bring back the mews for some people, keep it going for ourselves and anywhere in between for most people, and I think it's just something that's generally of now rather than the past."

Pam: "We don't try to think of it as a 60's revival particularly, I mean we've

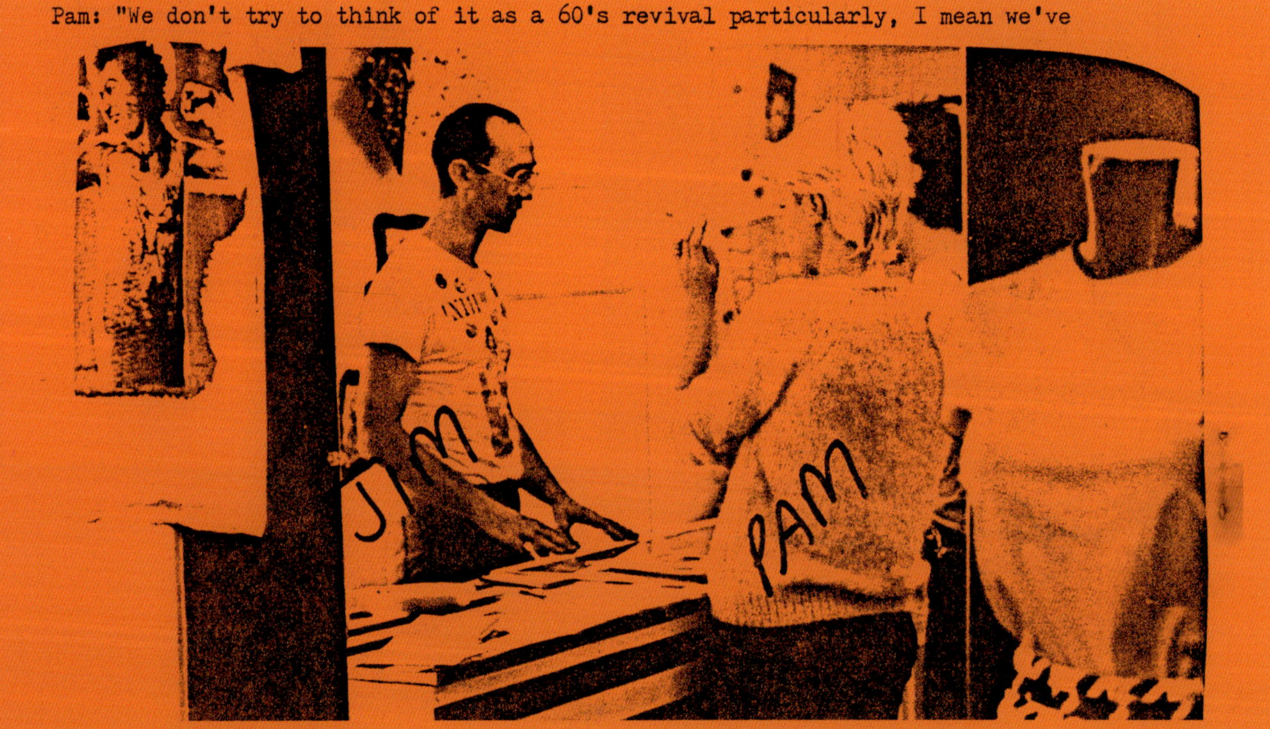

got shoes in here from England that they're still producing, but they've been producing them for 20 years, it's like classics style is how we think of it."

Jim: "There x are alot of styles that we think since we first started designing, since we met and worked together, that there should be certain styles as long as they are popular and suitable and should be available. I think there's too many things, like those shoes that Pam's talking about that went out of existance too quickly and too readily, and there's plenty of other styles that have been keptgoing that should never have been bothered with."

Pam: "We've found that the sort of styles we like come and go as far as the fashion industry is concerned. Sometimes we're the height of fashion because we do bright colors, sometimes we're not really out because brown is fashionable. We never use brown of gray or dull colors. It's very strange for us because we just keep doing the things we like and we're viewed differently as different styles come and go according to the industry."

Jim: "Yes, because although we like the classics we like things to change, and I think change is more important than keeping classic styles. I'd rather see everything changing constantly, that's what fashion is always thought of as, and I think it is, I think you wear clothes, you get bored with them, you want to change the quality and the style of them"

1978, "Fashion Fanzine"
Hollywood, Los Angeles
By kind permission of
Meredith Jacobson Marciano

MANIC PANIC, NEW YORK

"THEN WE OPENED THE FIRST PUNK STORE IN AMERICA. IT WAS JUST WHAT WE LOVED. WE ALWAYS SOLD WHAT WE LOVED, AND ALWAYS DID WHAT WE LOVED. SO WE GOT SO MUCH ATTENTION BECAUSE WE WERE THE FIRST PUNK STORE IN AMERICA, WE REALIZED WE WERE ONTO SOMETHING. IT WAS A GOOD THING."

Snooky

Tish, Snooky
Photo Glenn Brown
By kind permission of Manic Panic archive

In 1977, sisters Tish and Eileen (aka Snooky) Bellomo launched Manic Panic in St. Mark's Place, East Village, New York City. They had been sewing and reselling their own creations, when, with just $500, they opened the first punk style boutique in the USA. They specifically targeted punk rock and like-minded, alternative clientele.

Snooky: "We were the only ones selling that style in all of America. And so we had the jump on everyone. Then all these other 'punk stores' started popping up on St. Marks. Stores that had been vintage turned punk, but…we were the only punk 'owned and operated' store."

The boutique became an icon for 'first generation punk', due in part to the film *Downtown 81*, plus various film clips of the Ramones.

The two sisters achieved fame easily in New York City since they had been long embedded in the underground scene; they even sang backup on stage during Blondie's first shows at CBGB's and Max's Kansas City. They formed a band called Drop- Outs, and then a new group with Russell Wolinsky, Sic F*cks, which is still periodically active.

>
Tish, Gena and Snooky
Photo Glenn Brown
By kind permission of Manic Panic archive

At first, they sold vintage shoes with heels from the fifties and sixties and jumbles of clothes that were re-adapted, often made of sharkskin (a smooth, worsted fabric with a soft texture that has a two-tone appearance). They also sold sunglasses, gloves, and various bits of junk, all strictly vintage. There were also imports from England, especially the new and much sought after hair dyes.

Thanks to the sisters' background in the clubs, the press wrote reams on the two sultry sisters and their notoriety bloomed, so much so that soon they inaugurated their own Manic Panic line of cosmetics, offering hair colors to shock and creative tips of all kinds.

Their products soared in the late eighties, and the Bellomo sisters expanded well outside their small store, developing into a major international distributor by the nineties.

Manic Panic
Shop window
By kind permission of Manic Panic archive

>
1977, New York
Manic Panic, owned by the three young and enterprising new wavers; Tish, Gena and Snooky. The boutique not only sold original designs, but also vintage clothes from the fifties and sixties

CALLING ALL
PINHEADS
MANIC PANIC
33 St. MARKS PLACE N.Y.C.
Tel. 212-254-5517
OPEN
MON.—SAT.
1—8
FEBO
VINYL, RUBBER,
& LEATHER CLOTHES
STILETTO SHOES
TEESHIRTS
SLINKY PANTS
RECORDS, MAGS.
& R-N-R PICS
& of corse
X small HATS
OUR CLOTHES WERE DESIGNED
WITH YOU IN MIND!

TRASH
VAUDEVILLE
NEW N' ANTIQUE CLOTHING
TRASH
VAUDEVILLE
NEW AND ANTIQUE CLOTHING
TRASH

TRASH & VAUDEVILLE, NEW YORK

"THE ONLY OTHER PLACE
YOU COULD FIND STUDDED CUFFS
WAS AT A GAY LEATHER SHOP."

Jimmy Webb

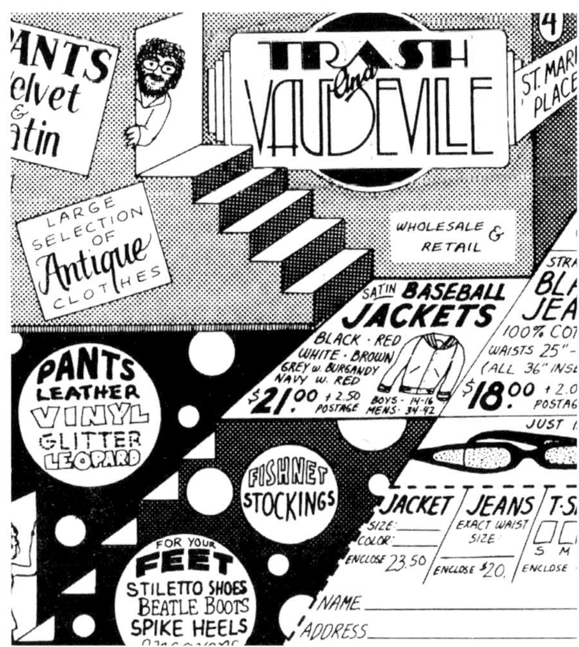

In 1975, Ray Goodman, a graduate of the Fashion Institute of Technology, opened the door to Trash & Vaudeville at 4 St. Mark's Place, Manhattan. Jimmy Webb, manager for one of the store's main clients, also ended up working there for many years. New York fanzine *Punk* would often advertise the store in its pages. Trash & Vaudeville sold velvet, spandex, leather and leopard pants, all sorts of shirts and badges, baseball jackets, shades, spike heels, Beatles boots, combat boots… The stock went on to be geared toward alternative youth culture: rockers, mods, punks, goths, rockabillies. When punk turmoil erupted on the British scene, Goodman flew to London and returned inspired; he started selling bondage trousers and all sorts of punk bric-a-brac. The store was regularly frequented by local rock legends like Patti Smith, Iggy Pop, Blondie, The Ramones, The Heartbreakers, The Dead Boys, and many others, contributing to its growing popularity.

10.1979, "New York Rocker"
Trash & Vaudeville
Publicity
(US magazine)

<< 1978, New York
Tom White of *Unnatural Axe*
Entrance of *Trash and Vaudeville*
Photo Richard Parsons

FREE KEITH RICHARD
EUROPE '78 TOUR

1978, New York
Trash & Vaudeville
Inside the store
Photo Richard Parsons

REVENGE, NEW YORK

This odd store was opened in 1976 on 3rd Avenue, Bowery, by Joseph Tomasello and Terry Jones, selling clothes and records. It was a one-of-a-kind store, coarsely painted and decorated. It boasted an aquarium, home to pet tarantulas looked after by *The Revenge Girls*. These young ladies sported hairstyles — Mohawks and the like in impropable colors — that were unnervingly cutting-edge for those days. Treated as a meeting point, the store was frequented by musicians and photographers from the punk scene, who lounged around on the large zebra sofa.

On weekends, people could stop for a 'punk makeover' before heading on to the famous CBGB club. A used shirt, torn and scribbled on, might only cost $3. For just $7, an improvised hairdresser would mess-up your hair — a great deal! *The Revenge Girls* gang (Ace, Barbara, Cheryl, Debbie, Eileen, Natasha, Pam, and Trixie) actually handcrafted many of the clothes on sale.

Revenge closed its doors in 1981.

1978, New York
Revenge
Store window
Photo Richard Parsons

>
1978, New York
Revenge
Pretty Pretty Punk Pam and Cheryl
Photo Richard Parsons

RAMONES
IS THIRD AVE

LIPS & LEOPARD

EDDIE KENT: DESIGNER

PHOTOS: MM

MODELS: **EDWARD ANDINO (L), EDDIE KENT**
CLOTHES: **EDDIE KENT**

I was brought up in rural Massachusetts. Out there Sears is the height of fashion. I started sewing when I was twelve. I had a natural ability. I remember my grandmother worked in a factory and she had this industrial sewing machine in her house that always fascinated me.

I first made doll clothes. Then I began making my sister the most outrageous outfits that my mother would never let her wear. She was about seven years old. They were miniature versions of the stuff I do now. I once made a leopard dress for her. I've always liked leopard.

After high school I went to a two-year design program in Norwood, the Henry O. Peabody School for Girls. I was the first man who went there. They tried to get me into tailoring men's clothes, and I almost bombed out the first year.

The next year I decided to do what I really wanted to do: glitter rock 'n' roll. My whole style is basically influenced by rock 'n' roll. Rock 'n' roll seems to be the forerunner of fashion. Any kind of theater dictates fashion.

I was raised a Jehovah's Witness. I was taught that rock 'n' roll is the devil's music. You weren't allowed to dance, no drinking or smoking. I didn't have a birthday party until I was eighteen. Now I have nothing to do with any religion. I believe in myself, even though I'll never forget all the stuff that was forced on me, three or four times a week until I was eighteen. Religion was never really scary to me; It was bizarre. It didn't make any sense.

After I got out of school I freelanced designing clothes for bands, and I washed dishes to support myself. I then got a job with Elliot Ness, which later became High Society. Last summer I worked in Provincetown at the Uptown Strutter's Ball designing things like crepe and drawstring pants and copies of vintage clothing. I work in a variety of styles, including wedding gowns.

People look at me a lot when I'm on the subway. It used to bother me, but it doesn't anymore. There's good reason for the way I look. I'm a designer, and I'm showing my wares. I think it's fun. As long as you have to wear clothes, why look boring?

But even before I was working for a store, I always dressed real crazy, even when I was fat. During the Nehru era I wore a pink satin Nehru jacket with gold buttons and pink elephant bells of brushed denim. They used to call me the pink elephant. (*MB/MM*)

EDDIE KENT, BOSTON

"I STARTED SEWING WHEN I WAS TWELVE. I HAD A NATURAL ABILITY. I REMEMBER MY GRANDMOTHER WORKED IN A FACTORY AND SHE HAD THIS INDUSTRIAL SEWING MACHINE IN HER HOUSE THAT ALWAYS FASCINATED ME.

I FIRST MADE DOLL CLOTHES. THEN I BEGAN MAKING MY SISTER THE MOST OUTRAGEOUS OUTFITS THAT MY MOTHER WOULD NEVER LET HER WEAR. SHE WAS ABOUT SEVEN YEARS OLD. THEY WERE MINIATURE VERSIONS OF THE STUFF I DO NOW. I ONCE MADE A LEOPARD DRESS FOR HER. I'VE ALWAYS LIKED LEOPARD."

Eddie Kent, *Subway News*, 1979

Eddie Kent made his debut as a tailor and window dresser at High Society, a high-end vintage clothing store. During leisure time, he designed clothes for private clients — unique, one-of-a-kind items. Some of his creations were exhibited in the shop, then through word of mouth they quickly become the main attraction. From 1977 to 1979, he used the basement of High Society as his laboratory; there he made custom-made punk clothes for local bands, strippers, and even prostitutes.

1978, Boston
Owner of High Society (left) with Eddie Kent
Photo by kind permission of Eddie Kent archive

<
1979, "Subway News"
(US fanzine)

1978, Boston
Store interior
Photo by kind permission of Eddie Kent archive

It wasn't so much a real store: it wasn't advertised; it didn't have a window; there was no sign. To enter, you had to have heard of it, to ring the bell and ask to enter. His creations were signed "Fashions to Boot." At the time, Eddie Kent was the first punk designer in Boston, a very conservative city. Eddie would stir up quite a sensation.

In the late seventies, he moved to New York to continue working as a designer for his own line, and there he founded the Garment District store.

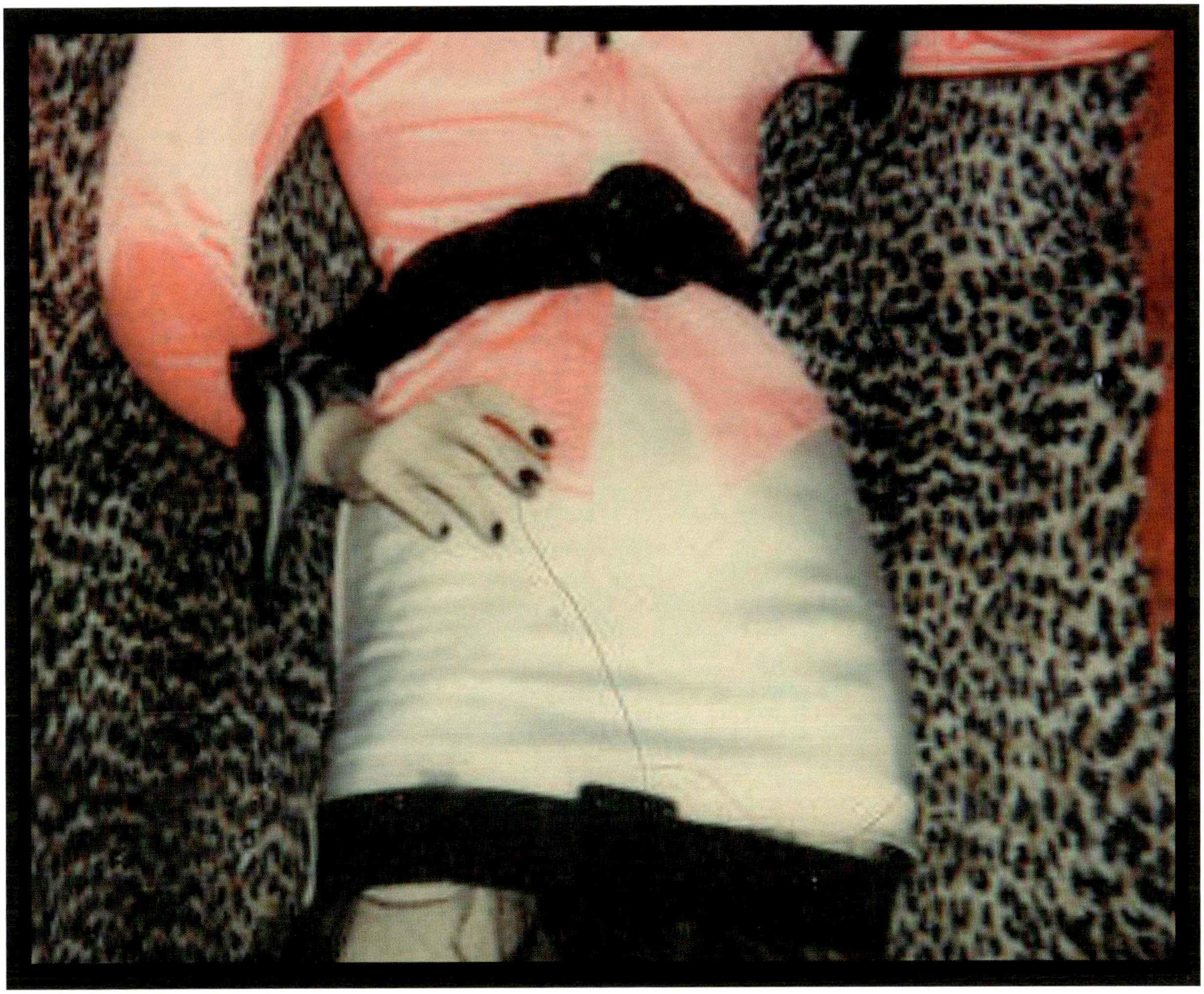

<

1979, Boston

A model wears *Fashion to Boot* with Eddie Kent
Photo by kind permission of Eddie Kent archive

1979, Boston

Fashion to Boot
Photo by kind permission of Eddie Kent archive

<

1979, Boston

"The all black outfit was one thing that I made many versions of. The pants were a very popular item. The fabric was a heavy weight stretch satin, that was created for making girdles. I bought all that I could find until it ran out."

1979, Boston

"Some of my one of a kind designs that were on display inside my store. I would change that mannequin every day and take pictures with my Polaroid camera."

Photo by kind permission of Eddie Kent

1978, Boston
Eddie Kent with friend Connie,
creator of silver jewelry.
Photo by kind permission of Eddie Kent

1978, Boston
At the store's entrance,
Newbury Street, Boston, MA
Photo by kind permission of Eddie Kent

ZIPPERHEAD, PHILADELPHIA

"ONE SATURDAY I TOOK A WALK TO ZIPPERHEAD / I MET A GIRL THERE, AND SHE ALMOST KNOCKED ME DEAD."

Dead Milkmen, *Punk Rock Girl*

In 1980, Rick Millan opened a shop at 407 South Street, Philadelphia. Although the store was launched a few years later than the others I have summerized, I want to mention it because of Millan's association with designer Raymond Ercoli. Ercoli's astounding contribution to the store began when he won the competition to decide its name: "Zipperhead." From that moment on, he became the outlet's official designer for its wares as well as creator of its weird and wonderful logos and flyers.

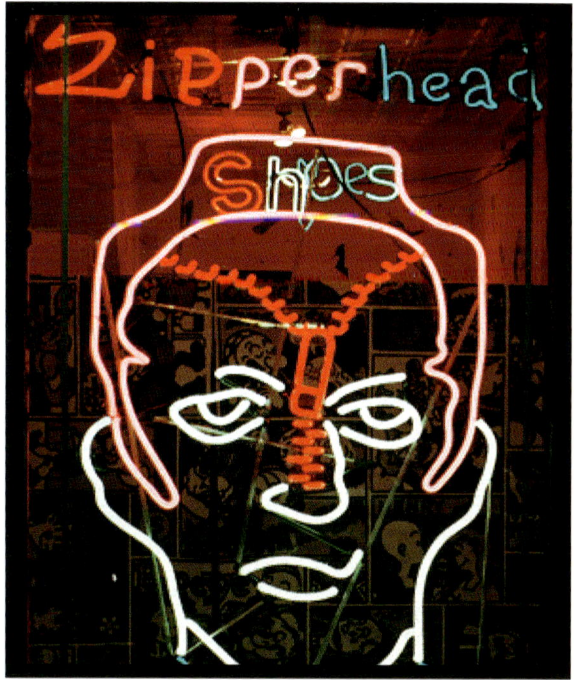

Neon Logo
Photo by kind permission of Rick Millan archive

"MILLAN, IN CASE YOU AREN'T ACQUAINTED, IS THE FOUNDER OF ZIPPERHEAD, THE 'ROCK AND ROLL TO WEAR' ALTERNA-STORE THAT SINCE 1980 HAS BEEN A CORNERSTONE OF THE SOUTH STREET SCENE. ZIPPERHEAD STUFF. I WON THE 'NAME THIS STORE' CONTEST, SO, YES, ADORING FANS, I NAMED 'ZIPPERHEAD'. I ALSO DESIGNED THEIR LOGO AND WINDOWS AND ADS SO IT WAS LUCKY I WON THE CONTEST!"

Raymond Ercoli

<
Cleopatra Liz Taylor
Logo by Zipperhead
Design Raymond Ercoli
Private collection

Printed T-shirt motifs
Design Raymond Ercoli
Skulls (left) | Tai Chi (right)
Photo by kind permission of Raymond Ercoli archive

The shop catered to a punk clientele, vending clothes and accessories. Ercoli's motifs blend lines and colors, ebullient patterns that wouldn't seem amiss in more 'casual' shop windows. They lack that provocative aggressiveness of the Brit brands in BOY and Westwood. The lightness of Ercoli's designs dallies with pop; its fabrics are closer to Fiorucci's, a bridge between punk and more commercial streetwear, a forerunner of eighties fashion.

Today, the façade of the shop remains: between the building's upper windows is a huge opening zip, invaded by giant ant sculptures that climb up towards the roof. It has become a sort of historical monument, alongside the Betsy Ross House and the Liberty Bell.

1981, Hand-printed motifs
Design Raymond Ercoli
Photo by kind permission of Raymond Ercoli archive

<
Zipperhead
Storefront
Photo by kind permission of Rick Millan archive

1981, Hand-printed motifs
Design Raymond Ercoli
Photo by kind permission of Raymond Ercoli archive

1983, Tinture
Design Raymond Ercoli
Photo by kind permission
of Raymond Ercoli archive

"WE WERE ON A CAMPING HOLIDAY AND GOT INTO LOTS OF TROUBLE. NO-ONE HAD SEEN PUNKS BEFORE AND IT CAUSED US LOTS OF PROBLEMS."

David Gwinnutt

Cleethorpes, Lincolnshire, UK, circa 1976-1977
Belle Dodds, Faye Dodds, Cass, David Gwinnutt, Chris Dodds. Photo by kind permission of David Gwinnutt archive

SEDITION TO US
MEANS TO SEDUCE
PEOPLE INTO REVOLT
AND THAT'S WHAT
WE'RE TRYING TO DO

Dame Vivienne Isabel Westwood

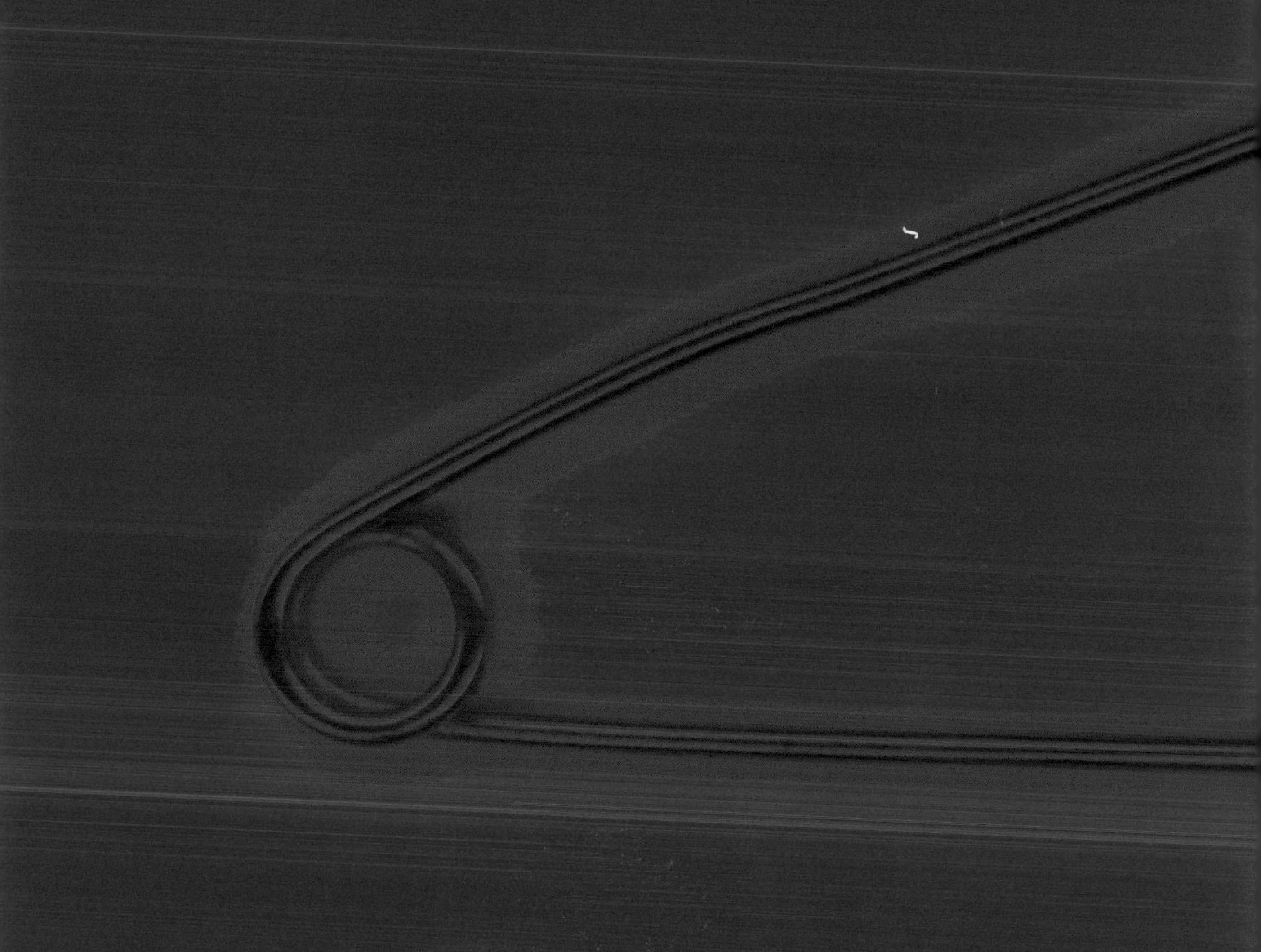

PROJECT
Matteo Torcinovich

ART DIRECTION & LAYOUT
Sebastiano Girardi, Matteo Rosso

ORIGINAL TEXT (ITALIAN)
Matteo Torcinovich

EDITING
Amanda H. Albano

TRANSLATION
James Sunderland

SUPPLEMENTARY TRANSLATIONS
English
Marta Zoppetti, James Sunderland
German
Maria Chiara Barbieri
Serbo-Croatian
Nataša Radovič
Russian
Carla Sabrina Marenco
Dutch
Pieter Jurriaanse

ILLUSTRATIONS
© Paola Querin pp. 70, 71, 72, 73, 74, 75

PHOTOGRAPHY
Cover © Peter Gravelle Generation X, The day they signed with
Chrysalis Records, 1977

© Edo Bertoglio — pp. 12, 14, 88, 164, 186
© Masayoshi Sukita — pp. 16, 42, 43, 109, 110, 130, 188
© Simon Barker (aka SIX) — pp. 20, 52, 128, 131
© Peter Gravelle — pp. 22, 46, 47, 48, 102, 140, 171
© Meredith Jacobson Marciano — pp. 25, 76, 78, 79, 80, 126, 166, 212, 214, 215
© Esther Friedman — pp. 28, 29
© Harry T. Murlowsky — pp. 40, 124
© Igor Moukhin — pp. 41, 82, 84, 85, 86, 87
© Robyn Beeche — pp. 54, 136, 137, 138, 139
© Jimmy Jocoy — pp. 90, 91, 104, 105, 125, 127, 178
© Richard Parsons — pp. 112, 113, 158, 223, 224, 225, 226, 227
© Dino Ignani — pp. 116, 117, 120
© Antonio Carmelo Erotico — pp. 118, 119
© Miss Lyn Cardinal — p. 125
© David Gwinnutt — pp. 132, 133, 134, 135, 172, 244
© Nazim Mustafaev, Russian Virtual Shoe Museum — pp. 146, 147, 148, 149, 150, 157
© PunkPistol Collection — pp. 156, 192, 193, 194, 195, 196, 197, 198
© George DuBose — pp. 174, 175
© Andy Sotiriou — pp. 200, 201, 202, 203
© Eddie Kent Archive — pp. 229, 230, 231, 232, 233, 234, 235
© Raymond Ercoli Archive — pp. 236, 238, 239, 240, 241
© Rick Millan Archive — p. 236
© From WET magazine — pp. 57,60 with the permission of Leonard Koren

THANKS TO
Edo Bertoglio, Masayoshi Sukita, Aki Sukita, Simon Barker, Peter Gravelle, Meredith Jacobson Marciano, Esther Friedman, Harry T. Murlowsky, Igor Moukhin, John Holmstrom, Jack Beeche of Robyn Beeche Foundation, Leonard Koren, Paola Querin, Jimmy Jocoy, Emma Daly, Richard Parsons, Dino Ignani, Repubblica di Frigolandia, Miss Lyn Cardinal, The Boston Groupie News, David Gwinnutt, Nazim Mustafaev of Russian Virtual Shoe Museum, Simon Easton of PunkPistol Collection, Ben Westwood, Richard Parsons, George DuBose, Andy Sotiriou, Mark Ciaramella, Gooby Gash of Manic Panic archive, Eddie Kent, Rick Millan, Raymond Ercoli, Marta Zoppetti, James Sunderland, Maria Chiara Barbieri, Nataša Radović, Carla Sabrina Marenco, Pieter Jurriaanse, Mattia Toffolo, Ludovica Polo.

GRAND OPENING!!
DEC. 10TH '77
1 P.M. ~ 6 P.M.
Tiger Rose
虎薔薇
NEW! PUNK FASHION
5257 MELROSE AVE. AT VAN NESS AVE.
LOS ANGELES, CA. 90038
TEL (213) 469-8359
FROM TOKYO SLASH
極楽鳥
GOKU RAKU CHO
総発売元 (03) 478-1859

"WELCOME BACK
DIAMOND LIL'S
FASHIONS of the Times - Clothes of the Century.
1487 PINE AT POLK - 771-6178
OPEN MONDAY - SATURDAY 12:00 TO 6:30 PM
LYDIA!!"

OH LEATHERETTE

Street Scenes
and
Other Dreams
clothing from
BLUE
GARDENIA
222 w burnside portland
226-0136
mon-sat 11-6

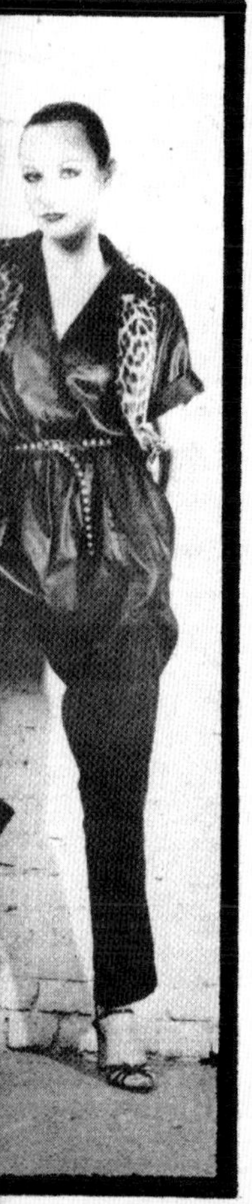

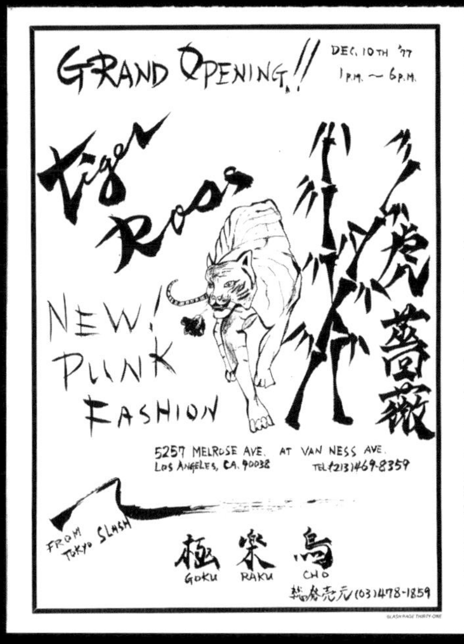

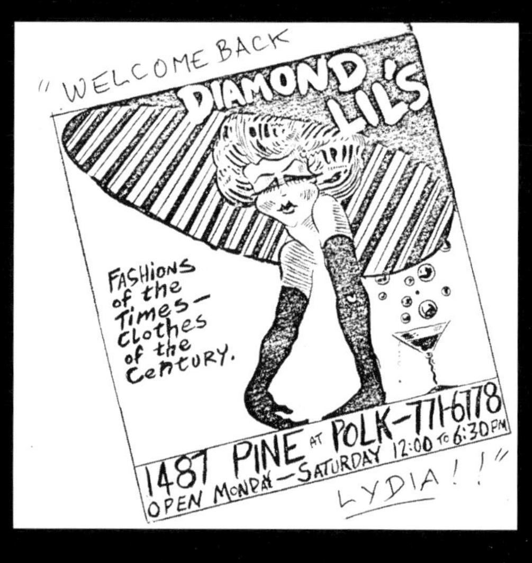

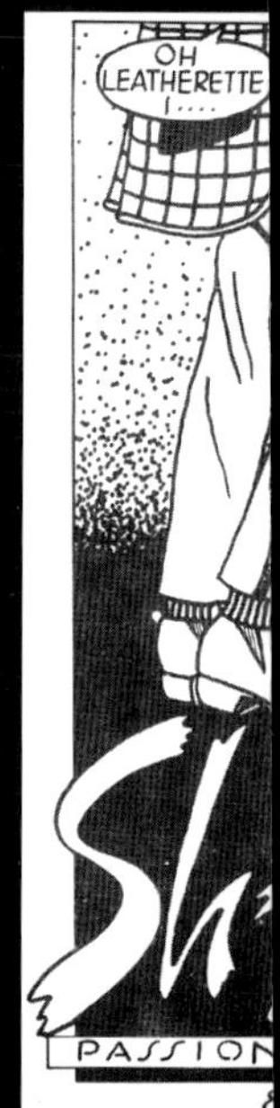

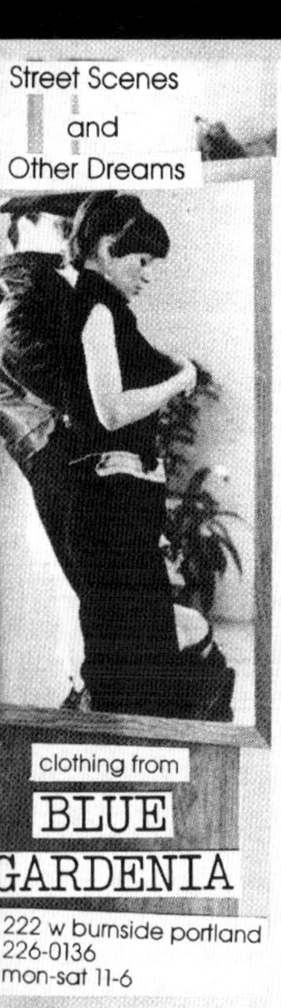

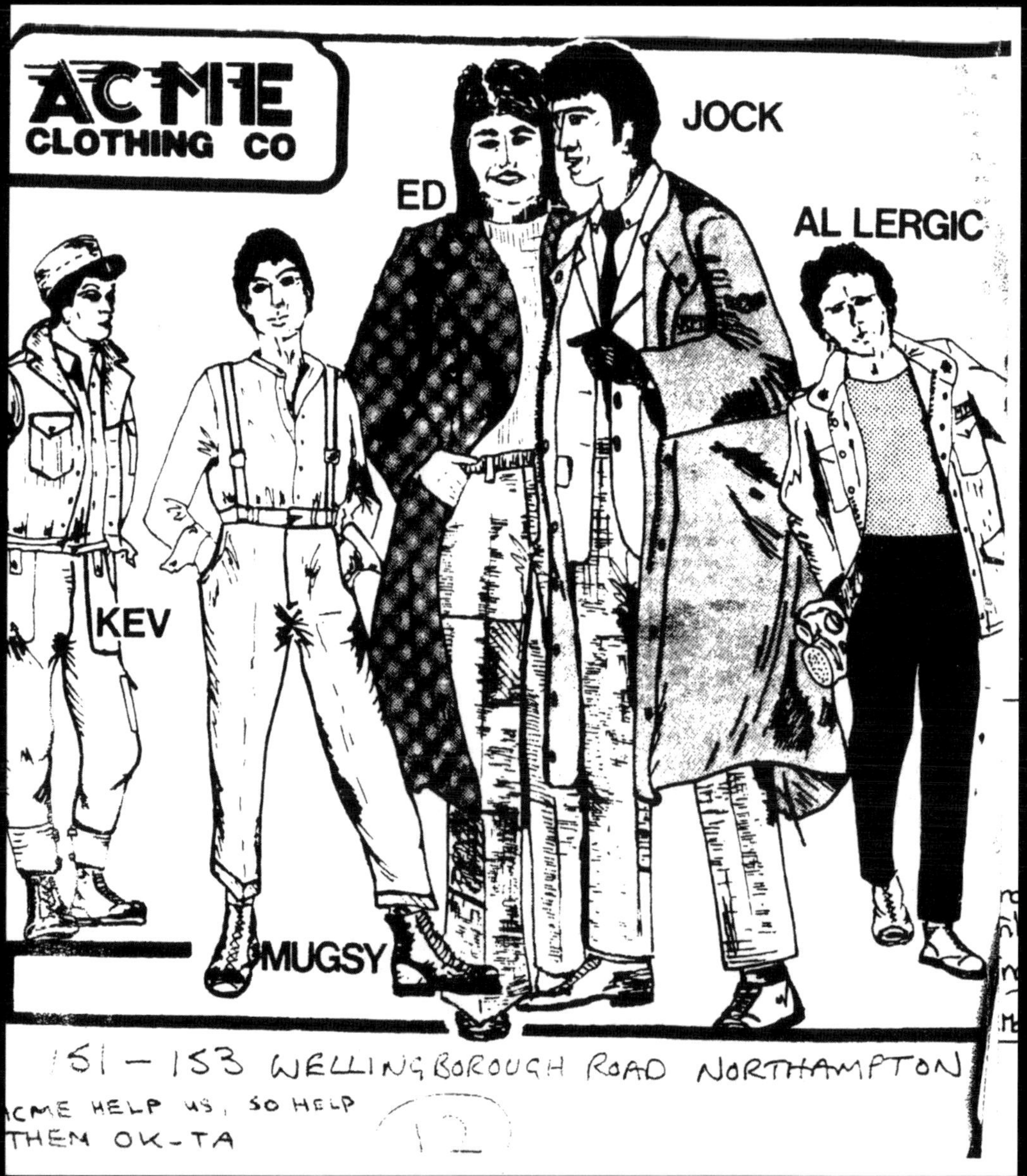

ACME
CLOTHING CO
JOCK
ED
AL LERGIC
KEV
MUGSY
151 - 153 WELLINGBOROUGH ROAD NORTHAMPTON
ACME HELP US, SO HELP
THEM OK-TA

TELL ME
s brady

SH-BOOM
WHOOSH!
SHAZAM!
WHAM!
BANG!
SH-BOOM
6 BRADY OFF MARKET NEAR 12TH IN SF
863-6646
PURE FASHION FOR OUR GENERATION
PUNK • POP • ROCKABILLY CLOTHING FOR MEN + WOMEN

GOOD COATS THESE
BLACK or NAVY
MELTON OVERCOATS
RED LINING & PARROT
£27.50
INC. P.&P.
SIZES 32"-42"
CHEQUES-P.O.s- TO:- THE ALIEN
20, CORPORATION ST., BOLTON. LANCS.
ALLOW 10 DAYS DELIVERY-ENGLISH MADE

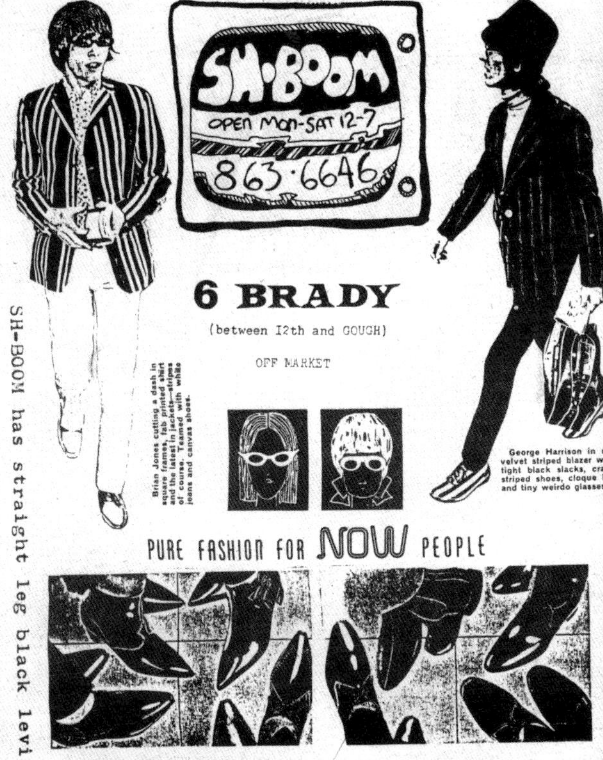

SH-BOOM
OPEN MON-SAT 12-7
863-6646
6 BRADY
(between 12th and GOUGH)
OFF MARKET
George Harrison in red velvet striped blazer with tight black slacks, crazy striped shoes, cloque hat and tiny weirdo glasses!
PURE FASHION FOR NOW PEOPLE
SH-BOOM has straight leg black levi's!
PUNK and POP FASHIONS FOR MEN and WOMEN

COSTUME FOR PARANOIAC DOLLS
Binmei.Flower.Essence.
☎463-5061 PM1:30-PM7:30 closed on WED.
SHIBUYA
2F 1GOKAN
MARUEI BLDG.

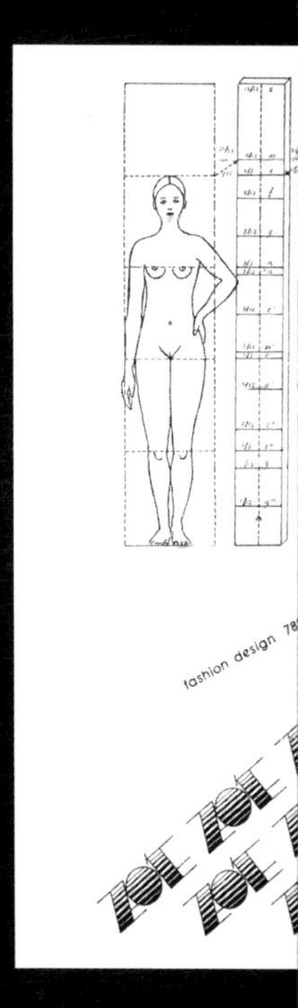

fashion design

snow dragon 2140 n. halsted
(312) 549-3772
wed - sun 1-9 pm
FASHION VICTI
AND OH . . . HOW IT CLINGS!
Now look, honey—you take Pepto-Bismol. Hospital tests prove it relieves upsets. It's wonderful for indigestion or nausea
viously, the lady doesn't know
FASHION FOR THE FUTURE...

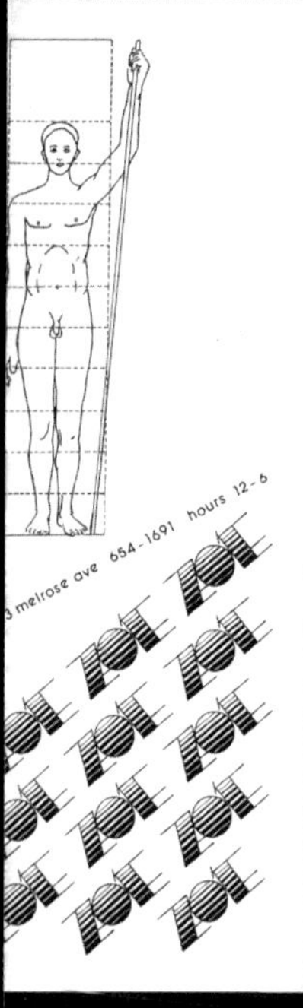
melrose ave 654-1691 hours 12-6

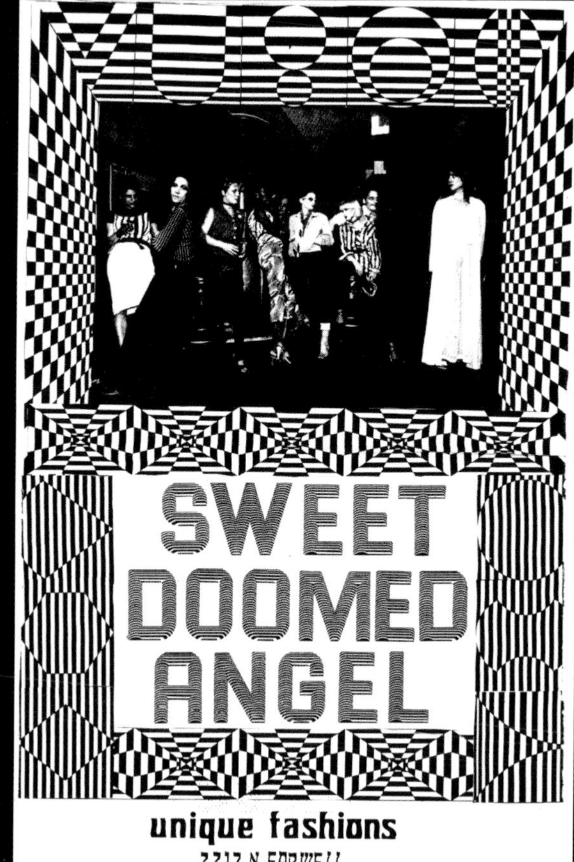
SWEET
DOOMED
ANGEL
unique fashions
2217 N FARWELL

PARALLEL LINES
66
MOUNT
PLEASANT
LIVERPOOL 1
OPENING
THURSDAY 12TH APRIL

KOOKY
CLOTHES FOR THE CLASSICALLY WEIRD
#741 Tulip Dress by
Elegant, seductive evening dress.
Low V-neck cut with high slit
Cotton-lycra rib
Color: black
One standard size
$ 93.95
#719 Netty tulip top
Low cut top with transparent
net sides. Very alluring.
Cotton-lycra
Color: black
One standard size
$ 64.95
#711 L.U. pants
skin tight leggings with
lace up ankles.
Cotton-lycra
Color: black
Sizes: S. M.
$ 44.95
#777 Corset top
tight body with full puff
sleeves. Adjustable laces in
the back. Shoulder pads
Cotton-lycra. Color: black
One standard size
$ 79.95
#776 Cube pants
houndstooth pattern
Cotton-lycra.
Color: checkered black&white
One standard size
$ 44.95
719
711
741
777
774
776
605
kooky [kOOki] adj (coll) very up-to-date and sophisticated; eccentric or bohemian in fashion, unconventional, unpredictable.
#774 Stripey scoopy top
form fitting Cotton-lycra top
with traditional
pattern. Color: black & white
Sizes: S.M
$ 49.95
#605 Kilt mini
shiny cotton-lycra with
leather & laces on waist
Color: black. Sizes: S.M.
$ 84.95
A new line designed by KOOKY London exclusively at BOGE

DRESSED TO KILL
451
455
141
ALL OUR PRICES INCLUDE SHIPPING & HANDLING !!!
450
724
725
ORDER TOLL FREE 1-800-YO BOGEY

MODERN CLOTHING

INDIVIDUAL TRADING COMPANY

SWEATSHIRT

As illustrated. Black & white panels. Please state size

£6.99

MOD BOATING BLAZER

Narrow Lapel, Centre Vent, 3 (metal) buttons. Sizes SML. Colours 1) Blue, red & white, 2) Grey, red & blue, 3) Maroon, navy & green

£24.95

FLAGS

UNION JACK TARGET CHECKED

All cotton flags approx 18" x 36"
£3.00 each or 2 for £5.50

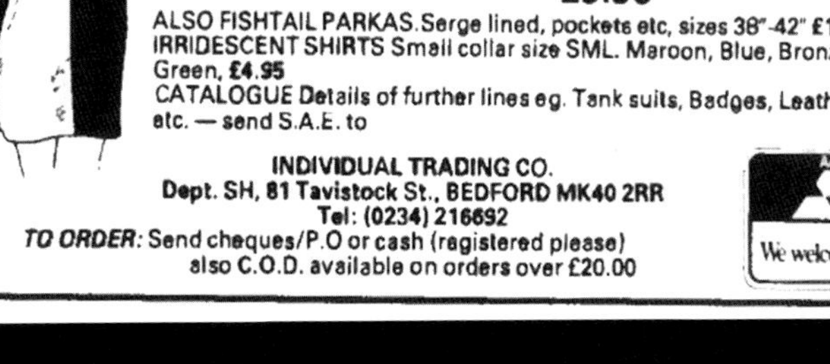

MOD DRESS

In black & white only.

Sizes 10/12/14

£13.95

MINI SKIRT

Black & white checked Mini Skirt as illustrated or smaller "Counterpane" check. Please state size

£9.95

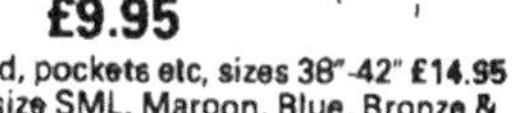

ALSO FISHTAIL PARKAS. Serge lined, pockets etc, sizes 38"-42" £14.95
IRRIDESCENT SHIRTS Small collar size SML. Maroon, Blue, Bronze & Green, £4.95
CATALOGUE Details of further lines eg. Tank suits, Badges, Leather jeans etc. — send S.A.E. to

INDIVIDUAL TRADING CO.
Dept. SH, 81 Tavistock St., BEDFORD MK40 2RR
Tel: (0234) 216692

TO ORDER: Send cheques/P.O or cash (registered please) also C.O.D. available on orders over £20.00

We welcome Access

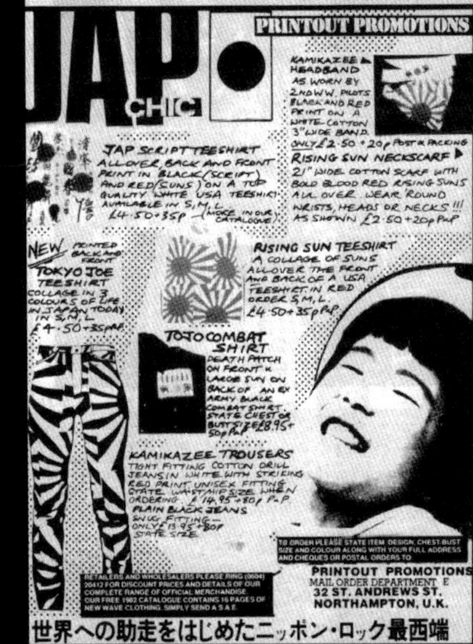

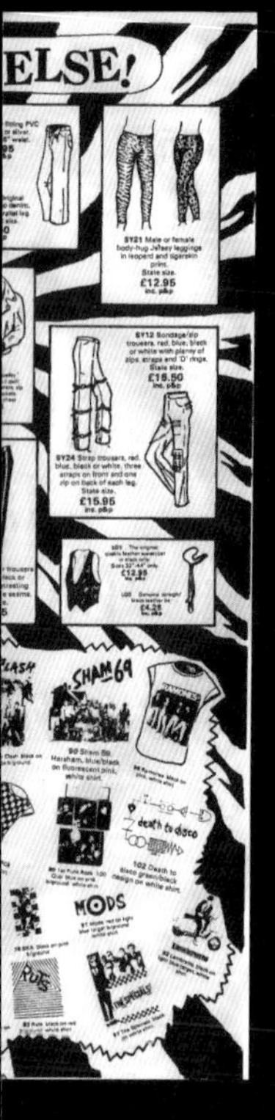

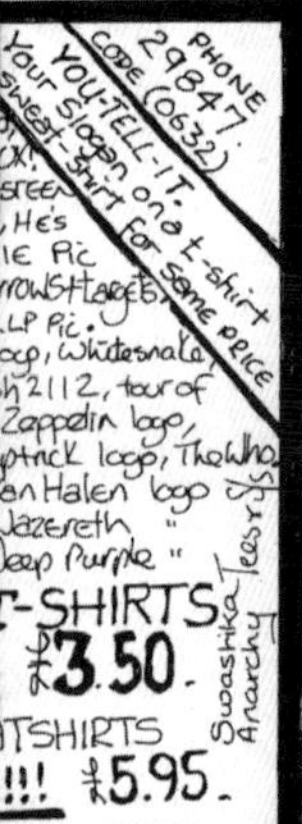

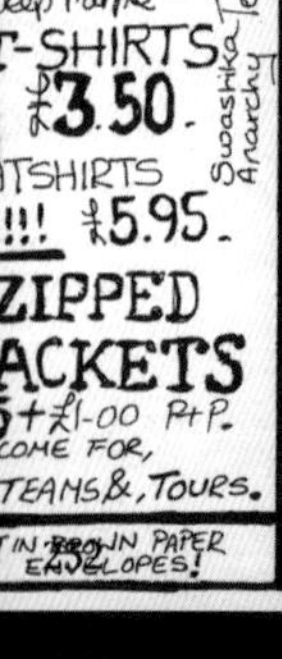

CALLERS WELCOME FRIDAYS & SA

BONDAGE JACKET Lots of zips and pockets in Black Drill Small, Med, or Large £12.90 + 60p P&P	CLASH JEANS Bondage style. Lots of pockets or zips. Colours Black, Red, Grey. Sizes: Men's 24" to 38", Girls' 8 to 18 £9.90 + 60p P&P
P.V.C. STRAIGHTS Colours: Black, White, or Pink. Sizes: Men's 24" to 38" Girls' 8 to 18 £6.90 + 60p P&P	

Money back guarantee if goods are returned un cheques, P.O.'s to:

MAINLINE (H), 51 TWO MILE HILL ROAD, KINGSW

DEVO

BUTTONS OF:

BLONDIE... CLASH...

DEVO.... DURY... CHE

ENO... GENESIS...

HENDRIX... ROCKY

PATTI... JAM... SEX

PETTY... RAMONES...

DISCO MAKES ME SICK... SID

FUNKY BUT CHIC... ROCK 'N' ROLL

TALKING HEADS.... hundreds

BERNIE

BOX 51

King of Prussia,

YELLOW DEVO CHEMICAL SUITS – $15.00 p.p.

ONLY

OTORBIKE JACKET

n Black P.V.C.
es: Small, Med, or Large
£12.90 + 60p P&P

L STRAIGHTS

: Black, Grey, or Red.
s: Men's 24" to 38"
Girls' 8 to 18
.90 + 60p P&P

7 days. Send

TOL, BS15 1BS

Fully lined Leopardskin (fur fabric) jackets.

ONLY £32.99

OTO

ALL BUTTONS: $1.50 pp

CARS... CRAMPS...
K... ELVIS C....
... R. GORDON...
OR... IGGY...
S... PIL ....
. ULTRAVOX...
Y... ROCK 'N' ROLL NIGGER
E....

HAND DESIGNED! FREE CATALOGUE! PHOTOS AVAIL.!!!

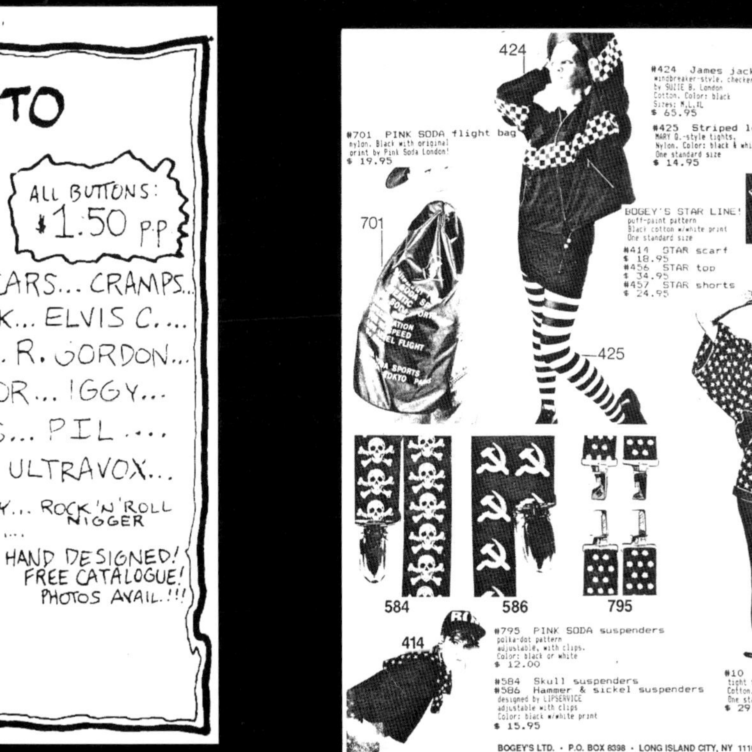

TRADE ENQUIRIES MOST WELCOME
NEW!
PRINT TROUSERS
BRIGHT RED TROUSERS WITH GROUP NAME ON EACH LEG (SAME GROUP NAMES AS TEES) COMPLETE WITH BONDAGE STRAPS & D-RINGS. A BARGAIN AT £15.95 + 80p P+P
PLEASE STATE SIZE
NEW!
STUDDED JEANS
SUPER FITTING JEANS WITH A ROW OF POINTED STUDS ON EACH LEG ONLY £15.95 + 80p P+P
RED OR BLACK
PLEASE STATE SIZE

GRINGOS - 1980 SALE
LEATHER JACKETS
KILTS
LEOPARD AND TIGERSKIN LEGGINGS
STRAP TROUSERS
BONDAGE TROUSERS
CONDUCTOR TROUSERS
TARTAN TROUSERS
BONDAGE 'T'
BONDAGE SHIRT
ZIP 'T'
CROMBIE
PARKA
TWO-TONE TONIC
LEVIS
SHAGGY JUMPERS
LEATHER WAISTCOAT & TIE
P.V.C. JEANS
CHECKED SWEAT SHIRTS
SALE
NEW

trEaTmeNt
clothing
32 GLENMORE rd

MOD BOATING BLAZERS
BLACK & WHITE GENTS SUIT
BLACK & WHITE MODETTE SUIT
MOD DRESS
£13.95
SKI PANTS
£12.95
PEDAL PUSHERS
£13.95
SWEATSHIRTS
£21.00
Also many other lines
FLAGS
Individual Trading Company
81 TAVISTOCK STREET Dept S BEDFORD MK40 2RR
TO ORDER

BUZZCOCKS
rock spirit fashion shop
SALE!
6/3〜18日

SUITS
T'SHIRTS
£3·50
GRINGO
Casuals Company,
39, St. Cuthberts Street,
Bedford, Beds.
CODE
SIZE
COLOUR
ALTERNATIVE
NAME
ADDRESS

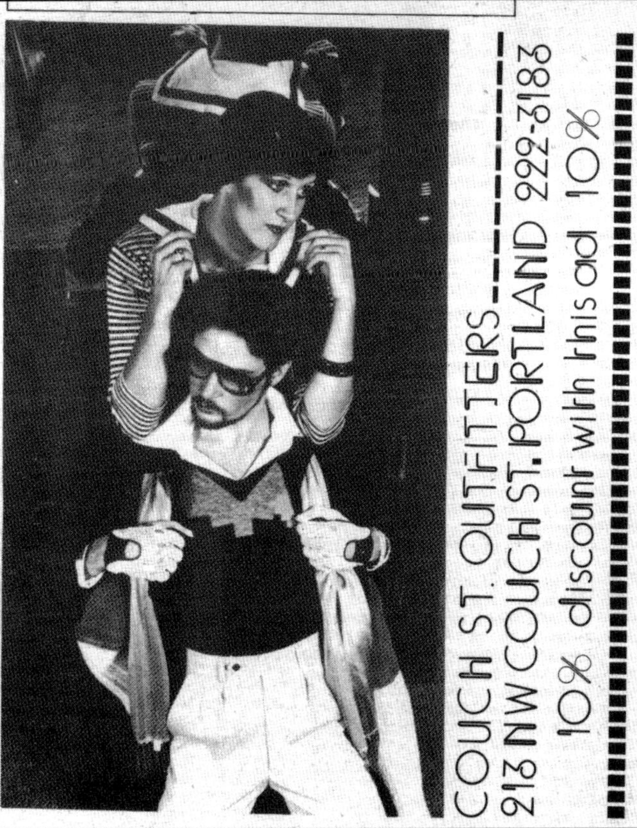

COUCH ST. OUTFITTERS
213 NW COUCH ST. PORTLAND 222-3183
10% discount with this ad 10%

LUTHER BLUE
FUTURAMIC
716 Columbus ave. S.F. Cal. 415 477-50
MODERNWEAR
DAY-GLO OBJEX • 80s FABRIX

"IN" RECORD STORE
WELL, YA GOT ANY A THESE? YET???
GO 'WAY, KID YA BOTHER ME....
DEVO
VILE-TONES
SUICIDE
X RAY SPEX
WIRE
CLASH
88 DISCO HITS AS SEEN ON T.V.
IS THIS YOUR PROBLEM ????
TRY BLEECKER BOB'S
GOLDEN OLDIES
179 MAC DOUGAL ST.
NY NY 10011
212-475 9677
LOTSA NEW WAVE X-CLUSIVES; THE HARD TO FIND STUFF; THE CREMÉ DE LA CREMÉ !!!!
IF YOU'RE NOT IN NYC, GIVE US A CALL
WE'LL HOLD 'EM FOR YOU.... AND MAIL EM TO YA!
OPEN 7 DAYS; TILL 1 AM; FRI & SAT TILL 3 AM!

make up Tracy ; model Susan
photo will donelly

© Copyright by Nomos Edizioni, 2019
First published in Italian language in 2019
Original Italian title:
Punkouture - Cucire una rivolta 1976 - 1986

Published in 2019 by

Gingko Press Verlags GmbH
Schulterblatt 58
D-20357 Hamburg
Germany
Tel: +49 (0)40-291425
Fax: +49(0)40-291055
Email: gingkopress@t-online.de

Gingko Press, Inc.
2332 Fourth Street, Suite E
Berkeley, CA 94710
USA
Tel: (510) 898-1195
Fax: (510) 898-1196
Email: books@gingkopress.com
www.gingkopress.com

ISBN: 978-3-943330-34-2

Printed in Poland